# YOUR BEST JUDGE IS YOU

A BOOK ABOUT YOU

HOW PEOPLE JUDGE YOU.

AND

HOW TO STOP LOOKING THINGS WITH THE BORROWED EYES.

AND

WHY YOU ARE YOUR BEST JUDGE

Seema Singh

**First published in 2016 by Seema Singh**

**BecomeShakespeare.com**
Wordit Content Design & Editing Services Pvt Ltd
Newbridge Business Centre, C38/39,
Parinee Crescenzo Building, G Block,
Bandra Kurla Complex, Bandra East,
Mumbai 400 051, India
T: +91 8080226699

**Copyright © 2016**
All rights reserved. Any unauthorized reprint or use of this material is prohibited. No part of this book may be reproduced or transmitted in any form or by any means, electronic or mechanical, including photocopying, recording, or by any information storage and retrieval system without express written permission from the author/publisher. Please do not participate in or encourage piracy of copyrighted materials in violation of the author's rights. Purchase only authorized editions.
Copyright © 2016

**ISBN 978-93-52017-34-8**

**Disclaimer**

The names, dates, places, events, and identifying details have been changed, invented, and altered for literary effect. Any resemblances to any actual person, living or dead, events, or locales are entirely co-incidental.

No part of this book may be reproduced or utilized in any form or by any means, electronic or mechanical including photocopying, recording or by any information storage and retrieval system, without permission in writing from the author.

*Dedicated to, the most merciful, The Almighty.*
*With thanks to – Reena & Dharmendra Yadav.*

# *TABLE OF CONTENTS*

| | |
|---|---:|
| 1. The story behind the story | 7 |
| 2. Why we judge | 15 |
| 3. Love your neighbor as yourself | 25 |
| 4. How People Judged On The Day You Were Born | 30 |
| 5. How people judge your past | 34 |
| 6. How people judge your Appearance | 47 |
| 7. How people judge your Weight | 54 |
| 8. How people judge others Religion | 59 |
| 9. How people judge your Profession | 60 |
| 10. How people judge your Clothes | 75 |
| 11. How people judge your Marriage | 82 |
| 12. How we judge ourselves | 86 |
| 13. What is your way of defining these? | 92 |
| 14. How parents judge you | 110 |
| 15. How teachers judge you | 120 |
| 16. How siblings judge each other | 128 |
| 17. How neighbors judge you | 132 |
| 18. How friends judge you | 137 |

19. How love interest or spouse Judge you     141
20. How God judges you     145
21. Why you are your best judge     162
22. What would be your judgments on these situations?     184

# *THE STORY BEHIND THE STORY*

Every coin has another side to it. Every person has another side to him. Again, every event has some untold story beneath it. To know the whole thing, we have to see the complete picture. We find a person to be arrogant and we quickly label him. It is the surface truth. On looking further, we find that the individual actually is an emotionally disturbed person. It's the disturbed person who is trying to hide behind the mask of an arrogant person. Earlier the person was being perceived as arrogant and now the same person is being recognized as emotionally disturbed. It is the whole truth. Between arrogance and pain, there lies a fine line. What you perceive to be an arrogant person might actually be a wounded person. In other words, we see the arrogance but not the pain. Most of the people live on the surface. People only see the things that lie on the surface. The truth remains hidden. Unless you see the truth with the impartial eyes, you cannot arrive at the right judgment. The half story is easily visible to us, but the larger picture remains unseen.

*If we believe that being dusky isn't beautiful, then we would judge that dusky people are not beautiful.*

*If we believe that women wearing fashionable clothes are not moral, then we would judge a woman in fashionable clothes as immoral.*

*Again, if we believe that poor people always steal, then we would judge poor people as thieves.*

The way we see the things determines the way we would judge them. If I had an experience of a doctor cheating me with exorbitantly high fees, I would judge all doctors as greedy. Just because one doctor tricked me, labeling all the doctors as greedy is certainly a gross injustice to all of them. Unless we take the whole picture into consideration, we cannot arrive at the whole truth.

## Surface truths, deeper truths

A surface level perception gives surface truth. A thorough understanding of things provides us with the more profound truths.

More deep the fact is, deeper the understanding it needs. Based on our ability to see things, we put labels on the people right or wrong, rich or poor, kind or cruel. Most of us cannot see beyond the eyes. The depth of a river cannot be estimated just by looking at the surface. Likewise, you cannot predict the exact nature of things, people or situations just by looking on the surface. People see something on the surface and immediately jump to conclusions. Such conclusions are just half the story.

It is wrong to say that poor people always steal. To the contrary, rich people can also commit stealing. Only a complete picture gives the whole story. Stealing has got more to do with greed. It has nothing to do with poverty or affluence. Based on our limited knowledge, we assume that a poor person has to be greedy, and a rich person has to be content. Often such assumptions are baseless. As the tip of the iceberg, the greater truth remains submerged.

*You are fat. You are tall. You are a fool.* These statements are half-truths. We might miss the point when we mistake a depressed person for someone who laughs too much without any reason. By laughing too much, the person is actually trying to mask himself. Without considering every detail, you cannot arrive at the correct conclusions. Everything is happening right in front of our eyes, but we fail to see the truth.

*Only with the impartial eyes, truth can be seen.*

## The tip of the ice-berg

*Shallow perception gives partial truth. Only an in-depth understanding would provide us the deeper truth.*

Surface truths are half-truths. Things on the surface are different from the things on the depth. As the major portion of the iceberg, the greater truth remains hidden. If a person willfully chooses to shut down his eyes to see the truth, then he is definitely missing the larger picture. The external appearance of a person, the difference in the cultures, the color of skin, and the gender, these are just the tip of the iceberg. The larger portion of the truth remains submerged. There is always more to a picture. A person's belief system, the surrounding atmosphere, the behavioral patterns, and the way of thinking, largely stems from the subconscious mind. Merely by looking at the surface factors we jump to conclusions. In the end, these conclusions may not be the correct. Shallow perception gives surface truth. In a hurry to immediately draw the conclusions, we miss the larger picture.

*We never know the whole story. There's always a different story behind a story.*

## How you judge this?

Consider this. A woman is seen in a figure hugging dress and wearing makeup. Whatever the reason for her wearing the dress; either she has worn the clothes as a part of the professional dress code, or out of her own choice to wear the particular dress. What is the general perception of a woman in fashionable clothes and makeup? It sounds unbelievable, but some people do not consider a lady in fashionable clothes as moral. The case might be categorically better in the cities where people readily accept women wearing fashionable clothes. The actual problem lies in the places where people still do not accept fashionable woman. People consequently label the woman as immoral.

Clothes in themselves do not make you less or more moral. A person is much more than the clothes he chooses to wear. Unlike many other things clothes are just the outer realities. Judging a woman by the way she chooses to dress is simply wrong. Clothes don't define morality. A person's choice of clothes has nothing to do with morality. A woman in figure hugging clothes can be as moral as any other woman.

Clothes don't define a person rather than the person wearing them defines them.

## Is this your story?

If you have a dusky skin and find that people do not accept you, what do you do? Do you want to change the color of the skin? You try all the fairness creams available, the herbal packs and the face packs available, and painstakingly apply them three times a day. The market is plenty of all types of fairness and cosmetic creams. The claims these creams make are astounding. Some creams promise to make you fairer within a month; other creams promise to make you better within a fortnight, and there are some creams that promise to do wonders in an overnight. It's good that these creams work to an extent. The actual problem arises when these creams don't work.

*Beauty is not in the face. Beauty is a light of the heart. – Khalil Gibran*

Each one of you is unique in your way. There is no need to be somebody else. It's strange that we don't accept ourselves. People with the dusky skin want to be fair, and those who are already fair want to be even fairer. In other words, everybody wants to become a better version of him. We judge beauty by the color of the skin and size of the body. Beauty means fairness. Real beauty is beyond the color of the skin or the size of the body. It has got nothing to do with the outer appearance. A loving heart, a caring attitude, a friendly behavior, and trustworthiness, are more important than the color of the skin.

Instead of channelizing all the energy into becoming fair skinned, why not channelize all the energy into finding someone who loves you truly. Why not search the one who loves you? True love is beyond the color of skin, the size of the body, and the amount of wealth. True love will go a long way. In the end, it's your ability to love someone matters. Love alone prevails. In other words, the way you perceive things will determine the way you believe.

## The truth, the false

In other words, what you think will reflect in the way you judge things. A narrow vision cannot give the complete truth. If you feel that people from a particular profession are greedy, you will judge all the people from the particular business to be greedy. Labeling all as greedy is certainly a gross injustice.

Consider this. Labeling all shopkeepers as cheaters because of one bad personal experience is certainly wrong. In other words, your belief determines your reality. I may believe that my son is the best; it is my held truth. It may or may not be the truth. Others might believe that their child is the best; it is their held truth. It may not be the truth. It's very clear that the same truth is viewed differently by different person. What one judges to be true the other judges to be false? Contrary to the people's belief system, the supreme truth remains unaffected. If you are able to see things correctly, you would see the whole picture.

*You are fat.*
*You are thin.*
*You are tall.*
*You are short.*
*You are dumb.*
*You are intelligent.*
*You have a nice sense of dressing.*

All the above constitute only half the picture. We are always busy looking at the surface. A good looking person need not necessarily mean a good hearted person.

## Is this your story?

Take this case. You are an engineer by profession. You have everything in life; a lucrative job, a six figure salary, and a comfortable living. Still, you find that something is missing. The inner satisfaction is missing. Engineering is your profession; teaching is your passion. You love teaching others. You especially love children. Educating the underprivileged is your dream. You would happily quit the nine to five job for a teaching job. It's your way of giving back to the humanity. To the contrary, the people around you and the family circumstances prevent you from pursuing your dream. You have no other option but to continue with the engineering job. The engineering job gives you money but not the inner satisfaction. The teaching job will give you emotional satisfaction but not money.

One day you are diagnosed with a life-threatening disease. You have only few months to survive. The hectic work load, the extreme stress, and the unhealthy eating, all together have taken a heavy toll. Enough is enough. You immediately resign from the job and leave for your hometown. You cut down all the ties from the outer world. No mobile phone, no e-mail, and no fax. All you want to do is to focus all your energies into fulfilling your last dream, to teach the underprivileged. You volunteer to teach the children at a local public school. The enthusiasm received is tremendous. The children are too happy to receive a teacher so well educated. The appreciation and the respect can be clearly seen in the children's eyes. The love and satisfaction and the cooperation you get here is totally heartwarming. If you had mustered up some courage earlier, you could have saved yourself from the after-effects of the previous job. Often, we learn the life's simple lessons the hard way.

An engineer is meant to carry an engineering job. A doctor is expected to carry a medical job. What would happen if all the doctors start building dams and all the engineers start doing surgeries? Wouldn't it be terrible? A woman who is happy being a home maker, we want to turn her into a chef. Again, a person who is glad to be a chef, we want to turn him into a manager. The bottom line is acceptance. Learn to accept yourself first and people would begin to follow soon.

## You can't escape being judged

Whatever you do, you cannot escape being judged. If you are rich, you would be labeled as a wealthy crook and judged for hoarding wealth. If you are poor, you would be judged for not being able to accumulate enough wealth. In other words, whether you are a rich or poor, you would be judged.

If you are a fat person, you would be labeled as an obese person and judged for putting on weight. On the contrary, if you are a skinny person, you would be labeled as a thin person and judged for being skinny. There is simply no way to escape. The vicious circle of judgment continues to affect everybody. If you are an actor, you would be judged by your acting. If you are a leader, you would be judged by your leadership. If you are a marketing guru, you would be judged by your ability to convince people. Again, if you are an office going person, you would be judged by your performance at office. In other words, no person can escape being judged.

If you are a married person, you would be judged by the success of your marriage. If you have children, you would be judged by the progress of your kids. In other words, nobody has escaped from being judged. If you are right, you would be judged for being right. If you are wrong, you would be judged for being wrong.

## Even great souls couldn't escape being judged

From the beginning of humanity till date, almost every great man has been judged for their teachings. Even the great men couldn't escape from being judged. The Buddha couldn't escape from being judged by his antagonist. Some people were fiercely against his teachings in the beginning. Jesus Christ couldn't escape from being judged by his antagonist. He faced crucifixion for doing nothing wrong. Nearly all great souls had to face judgment by people blinded with their limited belief and knowledge. In other words, even great men could not help being judged.

# *WHY WE JUDGE*

## Charity begins at home

The way we think, feel, and act, either has an effect on someone or has been affected by somebody.

We live in a society. The people have shaped our emotional being, whether directly or indirectly. The authoritative individuals who are in a position to control us like our parents, the teachers, and the elders, shape our thinking in a profound way. The teachings stay with the child forever. The children are greatly affected by those in the figure of authority. As a child, we felt vulnerable to those who taught us different things. A child absorbs almost everything that is present in his surrounding. A teacher scolds a child to make him take his studies seriously. It will have an immediate effect on the child. Since the advice to take studies seriously comes from a person in authority; it would compel the child to study harder. He begins to consider carefully. The early impression during the vulnerable stages of childhood stays with the kids. Children absorb our way of seeing things.

In some cases parents themselves teach their children, how to keep a tab on their neighbor's routine. I have seen children coming to their mothers and rewinding all the news of their neighborhood. When we find our children smoking a cigarette behind the door, mimicking our behavior, or drinking a cup of tea, we get angry with them. Children copy each and every behavior of their parents.

When the child catches us keeping an eye on our neighbor, he would learn the same. Like the mother who is peeping through the window, the child starts doing the same. The poor kid has no choice. The child starts doing the same. It is natural as the mold has already been set for the child. Like a pre-set oven, the child gets all the necessary training from his parents.

## The grass is greener on the other side

It's human nature to consistently evaluate things. We work tirelessly to judge the people around us and the circumstances of our lives. The reason for this constant scrutiny is very evident. We judge things and never try to find the truth ourselves. We always feel that the others are more happy, wealthy, and contented than we are.

The *yardstick* for excellence is the recommendations from the others. We never try to find out the truth ourselves. We never understand the value of our own feelings. It's strange that how much we are dependent on others for choosing us a house, a job, or a relationship. We are more interested in knowing about others than ourselves. We think that if our neighbor has bought something from certain store, it ought to be nice. If our neighbor has dined in a particular restaurant, the food would be nice. If our neighbor's children go to a particular school, the school must be nice. Why? What people think, feel, and say about us, matter more than what we feel ourselves. *We follow others, and we teach our children the same.* We diligently monitor our children. We want our children to go to the same school as that of our neighbor's children. We want our children to excel over the other students in academics, sports, or the extra-curricular activities. The yardstick for excellence is the other people.

We become blind followers of others. Blindly following others would lead to disastrous results. What matters is what people have to say about us. It leads to a sad turn of events. What works for one person may not work for the other. We learn that one of our friends lost 40 lbs of weight. It doesn't mean that we would be able to get the same result. The result may not be satisfactory.

## To feel good about oneself

It's human nature to judge. We can't help it. We evaluate people, things, and events on a daily basis. Each one of us has a different way of thinking. We think according to our mindset, the early conditioning, and the beliefs. Over a period, these beliefs become rigid in nature. And beliefs become hard to change with every passage of time.

*She is so fat* is a great way of telling ourselves that we are not *that* fat. We consequently begin to feel good about ourselves. It's a great relief to know that everyone is in the same boat. Judging others help us overcome our own guilt. It helps us to unburden. So, ultimately we begin to feel good about ourselves. *First, we hold on to beliefs. Later on, beliefs get hold of us.*

Some truths in the world are all pervading, never changing, and equally applicable to everybody. The sun, the moon, the earth, the planets, and every celestial object follow the same pattern of truth. Whether you go to America or India, the sun will rise at a given particular time. No matter where you live, no matter what you do, nature follows its own deadly pattern of accuracy. In other words, the greater truths in this world are strictly impersonal. Nothing can change them. They will eternally be the same. To the contrary, there are truths in the world that we have molded according to our needs. These truths change from time to time. We customize these truths as per our needs. If a person has held a belief in his mind that the earth is flat and not round, nothing can be done against that belief. Though we know the truth, we cannot make somebody accept the truth against their wish. We can do nothing about it.

Everybody loves their children, but to think that your kids are the best is partial perception. Partial perceptions lead to partial truths. You see the surface and immediately jump to conclusions. The truth will be truth. If we don't like a particular fact, we modify it to fit into our molds. Though we know that smoking is injurious to health, we bury it under the fact that everybody else is also smoking. Here we modify the truth to fit into our mold. It's because of this tendency that we distance ourselves from the greater truth. We live with the half-truth.

## To feel good about ourselves

The way a person talks, eats, and dresses, has either been influenced by others or by the person himself. It means that either we have affected others or we have been affected. We are highly interested in knowing about others. Deep lies a person who loves to flaunt. We want to be recognized. It is human nature.

Whether it's a new house, a new car, or a brand new watch, what's the point in having all these if there is nobody to admire it? It's only when people come to us and shower their praises, we begin to feel good about ourselves. Another aspect is that we imitate others. We are compelled to buy the same face wash, a leading actor endorses. Why? We want to feel good about ourselves.

Whether asked or not, a woman would tell everyone that her daughter lives in America. Why? It feels good when people come to know that your daughter lives in a well known country.

Whether it's your newly acquired cycling skill, achieving excellence in the yoga, or a recipe made to perfection, we want others to admire it. Telling things out of joy is not boasting. Sometimes we want to share our good experiences with others. We want to tell others that how good it felt; when we donated for a cause. How relieving it was to feed a hungry soul. It's the goodness you want to spread to everybody.

Whether you were being able to climb a mountain successfully for the first time, or you made a delicious pastry, or your child placed a fallen baby bird back into its nest, good things shouldn't be left hidden and must be shared. More and more people should come to know about the good things. Often, while telling about our accomplishments to others, the fine line between the arrogance and pride gets diminished. We want recognition. There's nothing wrong in it. The problem begins when the desire for admiration turns into attachment. We get attached to ourselves and our deeds. When people don't say or feel the things we want to hear, we get hurt.

## To assure that you are not alone

The man is a social being. We want to accept and be accepted in return. We don't want to be left alone. It's strange that when it comes to being promoted or receiving an award, people want only themselves to get awarded. When it comes to being scolded or being caught for a mistake, people want a company. It always feels great to have somebody by your side. Remember the day you were being sent out of the class? You felt relieved when your classmate was sent out too. How relieved you felt. Remember the glass window that was broken because of you. Someone else came to your rescue and you felt unburdened.

Nothing gives more relief to know that your neighbor's child has also failed in his exam like yours. It's a solace to know that you are not alone in the boat. There is someone by your side. It feels good to know that you are not alone. It brings peace that everybody is sailing in the same boat.

It's human nature to feel relieved when somebody is there by your side. Though there is someone by your side, still, you cannot escape the consequences. Other people cannot take your burden of guilt on their shoulders. You alone have to suffer your guilt. Nobody else can help you in this matter. Whether it's a scolding from your mother, being caught for lying, or being caught eating during dieting, it's always a huge relief to have someone by your side. Two is always better than one. It always feels better.

A woman would ask one particular question to everybody she met. She would ask to people that how was their children's married life going on? When people would say fine, she would feel unhappy inside. When some said that their children's marriage was not doing well, she would feel relieved. On knowing the woman further, it comes out that her daughter was leading an unsuccessful married life. By asking people, she was actually telling to herself that she's not the only one leading a painful life. There are some other people along with her in the boat.

If I am happy with my life, what people are saying or doing won't interst me. The only time I get interested about others is when I am not happy with my life. If I am doing the right deeds, I won't be searching out for the other sinners. It's only when I have sinned; I would want to find another sinner to accompany me. The point is that one unhappy person would be searching another unhappy person for company. So, when you come across such individuals, instead of getting angry at them, try to be compassionate towards them, as they are already unhappy with themselves. If they would have been happy in the first place, then they wouldn't be busy searching another unhappy soul. The more compassionate you are, the more you would understand. It's because of people's own pain; people search others' pain. Only compassion can end this vicious cycle of sufferings.

## To feel less guilty

It's one of the major reasons for judging. We are humans and at some point in our lives, we all made mistakes. Naturally we felt guilty. It's because of these burdens that we judge other people. We want to check if others too, did something wrong like we did. If yes, how did they overcome it? It is relieving to know that you are not they only person to be on the wrong side of the track. There are a lot more people with you. We seek others with the similar traits like ours. The point is, what we are searching in others actually lies in us. Whether it's a self-harming habit, or a health issue, we want to have somebody by our side. Two is always better than one. Whether it's a willful neglect of health, a self-harming issue, or an overeating issue, we seek others having the same trait like ours. It's a relief to know that we are not the only one who is guilty.

*He smokes heavily.* It is a way of telling to ourselves; it's ok to smoke, as everybody else is doing the same. It lessens the guilt that is eating us from within. We begin to feel better about ourselves. In other words, we want to reduce the burden of the guilt. We never try to quit smoking. We try to seek other smokers for our company. Imagine one smoker helping the other. Is that possible? It's like one blind person leading the other blind person. Both would end up falling in a pit. It would surely lead to a tragic end.

*She is overweight.* It is a way of telling to ourselves; we are not the only one who is overweight. There are plenty of other people who are like us. It's ok to be who we are. It's ok to overeat. The point is, we become comfortable in living with our problems. We never try to eradicate the cause of the problem itself. We begin to think, it's ok that I am over weight, I am not the only one. There are many others with the same problem. We are trying to justify our problems and not attempting to correct it. This tendency leads to even more problems in the future.

*He drinks heavily.* It is a way of telling ourselves; we are not the only person who drinks. Many individuals are doing the same. In this way, we are shifting the blame onto the other person. We are blaming the other person for no fault of theirs. We started drinking on our own. Nobody forced us, but we blame others for our drinking habits. We justify ourselves by saying that we are not the only one who drinks. Everyone around us is doing the same.

*She is not beautiful.* It is a nice way of telling ourselves; we are indeed beautiful. By labeling others as not beautiful, we want to tell that we are beautiful. By labeling others as fat, we want to tell that we are not fat. Likewise, by labeling others as liars, we actually want to tell that we are not liars. In other words, we consciously try to figure our own insecurities in others. The thing is we are not in the search of others' insecurities, we seek our own insecurities. Once we get to know that everybody is in the same boat, we are happy for ourselves. In other words, we want to climb up by pulling someone else down. In other words, we are justifying by telling that everybody else is doing the same. In fact, we are trying to dilute the guilt that is eating us from within.

In the short run, we may feel good by blaming others for our bad habits. In the long term, we can't escape the consequences. Whether we like it or not, we have to face it alone. It's easier to find a company than to take the pain to change us. It's like searching another drug addict because we are one. We should have strived not to be a drug addict in the first place, but we didn't. We become an addict first and then search another addict so that we feel less guilty. We never try to eradicate the problem itself. We put ourselves into a problem first and then search others having the similar traits.

In other words, it's like one wrong person in search of another. Imagine one drug addict coming in support of another addict. What would happen? Both of them would end up creating more troubles for themselves. They would be creating more miseries. It never helps. Pain leads to even more pain. We never try to rectify our own mistakes; we search someone having done the same mistake like ours.

Learn from your mistakes. They teach a lot.

## To learn from others

We can learn many things just by an everyday observation. Why is that we always see the wrong things? Why can't we see the good stuff? We have become so accustomed to seeing negativity around us; we don't even bother to see the good things happening. We don't see the sunshine, the moonlight; we don't care to see the buds blooming, and the baby smiling. Often, we don't feel and hear our own heartbeats.

We have become so rigid in our thinking that we can't see the good things in the world. We can't see the goodness in people. The bright side often goes unnoticed. All our attention goes in finding the dark side of the people, things, and the situations. It's not that judging is always wrong. If positive changes happen, it's a welcome sign.

*I have learnt silence from the talkative. Toleration from the intolerant & kindness from the unkind. -Khalil Gibran*

We can learn so many things by obvious observation. Sometimes we think ourselves to be perfect in every sense.

When we find somebody with the same level of negativity like us, then we realize how hurtful we were to others. Sometimes to understand ourselves, we need to see with the others' eyes. In the pursuit of greater things, greater success, and greater glory, the little things goes unnoticed. The little things don't matter to us. The things we think to be unimportant. The things we don't care.

A dog getting hurt and bleeding in the middle of the busy road often goes unnoticed for the same reason. It happens because of our tendency to overlook the smaller things. Things that we find unpleasant in others, we can strive to change in us. Life often teaches the simple lessons. We insist on learning it the tough way. Negativity in others can teach us to become more positive in life. Somebody who often gets angry for the wrong reasons could teach us how it feels inside, when we used to do the same. They can clearly help us to realize, what it's like to be in the others shoes. How the other people felt, when we used to get angry for apparently no fault of theirs. We can clearly analyze our own behavior through others.

Do you remember seeing any movie? Have you ever felt that the character in the movie is related to you, in some way or the other? Did you felt that the character is playing your role? How it felt when somebody else plays our dark side. We don't like to see our darker side. Why? It's only when somebody else caused us the pain; we realized that how much pain we were causing to others. If somebody broke our flower vase, we immediately become angry. On other hand, when we break somebody else's window, we think it's not a big deal. Why?

It's no shame in learning from other people. Wisdom is wisdom. Have a deep introspection. You will find all the answers. A simple observation helps to find the unexplained answers. In the end, it's the willingness to learn from our mistakes matters.

# *LOVE YOUR NEIGHBOR AS YOURSELF*

**You shall love your neighbor as yourself. -The Bible**

We are being asked to love our neighbor as we would love ourselves. We have a different definition of love when it comes to loving ourselves and our family. And we have an entirely different definition of love when it comes to loving the people outside our family. How do we love each other?

*The whole world is one large family.* It's the love and peace that binds the people together. Though people may come from different countries, cultures, caste, creed, and diversities, the mother earth graciously accepts us. The sun, the air, the water, the earth, in other words, no force of the nature discriminates people. The sunlight is readily available to everybody alike; the air doesn't discriminate between people; the water quenches the thirst of anybody who drinks it.

In other words, no force of nature chooses to distinguish between people. God equally loves everybody. God never discriminates nor judges anyone. We are being asked to follow the God's footsteps. Love makes the world go around. Love transcends all the barriers, all the boundaries, and all the hatred.

Love wins everybody's heart. Love knows nothing about caste, creed, age, and wealth. Love rules the world. Remember when you are in love with someone, you forget all the differences; you don't ask their race, caste, or creed. You just love them.

When it comes to loving our family, we love them, no matter what the circumstances are. Is it not true that when it comes to loving our family, we have a different definition of love? And when it comes to loving others, we have a completely different definition. The point is, why has love to stop at the boundaries. The entire world is one great family. It's the love that binds us together. The boundaries of caste, creed, wealth, and gender are nothing but man-made. It's the people, who have created a division between people in the name of religion, caste, and creed. The Holy Bible asks each one of us to refrain from judging each other. In other words, we are being asked to rise above the things that cause hatred and division in the society. We are being asked to love one another. No religion has ever taught us to fight in the name of God. Still, we fight in the name of religion. We are being asked to love others; in the way we would love ourselves and our family.

## Except humans, nobody goes against nature

The squirrel is happy being a squirrel and the rabbit is happy being a rabbit. There are no conflicts in the animal kingdom. Everybody is meant to be the way they are. There is absolutely no need to be somebody else. It's the differences that make us count. Imagine, what would happen if all the flowers would want to be roses. Wouldn't the world be boring? It's the variety of flowers that make them beautiful. Each flower adds to the beauty of nature. Nevertheless, every flower is special. Likewise, you are special in your way. You need not pretend to be somebody else. There is absolutely no need. Each one of you is special. You require no effort to be yourself. It's because you are meant to be just you. For you, to be somebody else, you need to put in a lot of effort.

Being our self is easy. We think ourselves to be the most intelligent living being on the planet. Still, humanity has not been able to make peace with the self. We human beings are always in conflict; in some turmoil. We always want to get better, only to end up becoming nobody. We want to become this. We want to become that. It's so easy to be our self. The existence has made everything perfect. Life never makes a mistake. Everything is perfect in nature. All we need is a wholehearted acceptance.

*I am depressed.*
*I am a loser.*
*I am a dumb.*
*I am ugly.*
*I am fat.*
*I am a good-for-nothing.*
*I am an idiot.*
*I am nobody.*
*I would end up as a failure.*

All these judgments are nothing but the belongings of your own mind. The existence never judges anyone. It never puts labels on people like fat, thin, beautiful, ugly, bad, good, average, mediocre, intelligent, or dumb. Why do you want to be somebody else when it is so easy to be yourself? On one hand, you want to be effortless and on the other hand you are putting all your energies into proving something. You are pretending to be somebody else; in the end, an entirely different person is produced. The end results are contradicting. You only end up becoming a duplicate version of someone else. Imagine how would the world be if everybody wants to be like a celebrity? Wouldn't it create an identity crisis for everyone else?

## Nobody can judge you better than you do

*There is no court greater than our own conscience. - M.K.Gandhi*

Nobody knows us better than we do. Nobody knows about our ambitions, desires, and decisions better than we do. Leaning blindly on to others for our daily decisions may bring disastrous results. If left unchecked, the innocent looking habit of following others might lead to a disastrous turn at the later stage. There are many other things along with imitating the neighbors; our children learn from us. Of course, there is no denying the fact that the good things should be absorbed, no matter the source. Though there is no harm in learning the good things, the actual harm lies in not knowing where to draw the line.

Blindly copying someone would give disastrous results. You cannot lie to yourself. You know everything about yourself – the past, the mistakes, and the weaknesses. Still, when it comes to taking a major decision in life, you turn to somebody else. It's strange that we turn to astrologers or a future teller for our problems. There is nothing wrong in seeking help. But the problem is that the problem lies within you.

It's as the person who is to be treated is you, but the medicine is being administered to somebody else. Common sense tells that you should be taking the medicine. Isn't it? But, we hope to get fine by making somebody else consume the medicine. It's bizarre. If your shop is not running well, first have a deep introspection on why the shop isn't running well. It may be that your customer service is not as good as others. Maybe your products are not up to the mark. There could be a variety of issues. But we never stop a while to think over these issues. We immediately jump to conclusions that somebody else is harming us or may be an evil eye is casting its spell. In fact, the problem lies in us and the solution should also lie within us. Isn't it?

*Your best judge is you.*

Whether it's your personal decision or a collective decision, you cannot escape the consequences. Whether it's a family problem, a career related problem, or a health problem, nobody else can decide it better about what is good and what is not. When it comes to taking the important decisions in life, you turn to others for help. People decide what would be your name, the school you would go to, and the career you would choose. Again, it's the people who decide whom you should get married. There is very little of thing left for us. Everything is pre-planned.

Someone might argue that what's wrong in seeking advice. In fact, there is no foolproof plan to take the correct decisions. Anything could go wrong. Anybody could go wrong. You never had a mind of your own. You never made decisions of your own. Again, you never had judgments of your own. In the long run you will be the most affected. There is nothing wrong in seeking advice. But you cannot predict anything in advance. Anybody can get it wrong. If you are leaning too much on to others' for decisions, people would be responding as per their own experiences. There is always a possibility of getting things wrong

# *HOW PEOPLE JUDGED ON THE DAY YOU WERE BORN*

## Judging begins early

A baby is born. A family is complete. We dream many things for the baby. We will do this for the baby. We will do that for the baby. We shall raise our children in this way. The name of child is planned. The school, the college, and the entire career is planned. And in some cases, people even decide the future bride or bridegroom for their child. Everything has been set already. We already set a ready-made mold for the child. When the child is born, there is little work left for the child. And we can't wait enough for our baby to come in this world and to get molded as per our beliefs. Everything is preplanned. Do you remember the day you went to some naming ceremony of a child?

## How do you judge this?

*The baby is active.*
*The baby is healthy.*
*The baby is beautiful.*
*The baby seems to be friendly.*

*The smile of the baby is infectious.*
*The baby looks like his father.*
*The baby looks like her grandparents.*
*The baby looks dull like her mother.*
*The baby has a flat nose like her mother.*

## How would you judge this?

If a child is born with mental retardation, or any physical deformity, everybody around the baby tells to the parents that the child's hopes are not good. The way in which the baby is being judged is not good. Irrespective of whether one is an expert in the medical field or not, people are ready to offer their suggestions. People project the situation as if; it is the end of the world.

You can't control the people or their reactions towards you.

Out of concern or out of sheer ignorance, people might say hurtful things. But people are people. Negative talks lead to negative results. By indulging in negative talks, you are surely depriving somebody of his hope. No one is a born winner or a born loser. Instead of helping the child, we start giving our judgment that there's little hope. We are depriving a child who is already in need of help. If the foundation of a building is weak, the building is going to be weak. Every child is an asset to the nation. Every life is precious for the country. Proper care must be taken to ensure that every child gets equal chance to bloom.

## How do you judge this?

*The baby will never be able to walk on his or her feet.*
*Don't hope much for the baby. It's in vain.*
*The baby would be a good-for-nothing.*
*The baby will never be able to live up to your dreams.*

## Great soul who made the impossible, the possible

Helen Keller was an extraordinary soul who shined brilliantly by overcoming all extraordinary difficulties. She was deaf and blind. She overcame all the difficulties bravely and graduated. Helen Keller wrote many articles which were later published in a book. Helen Keller was a real inspiration. Incredible achievements indeed.

## Why childhood is a crucial stage?

Childhood is a crucial juncture. Whatever impression imbibed upon the child's mind stays forever. These perceptions play a significant role in determining the course of life. Whether these perceptions are right or wrong, the child absorbs everything. Knowingly or unknowingly, we subject the child to our limiting beliefs and judgments. Like a dry sponge, the child absorbs everything. In fact, the child doesn't even know the difference between right and wrong. It takes time to finally realize that every individual is different. The child should be loved enough at this crucial stage of life, but this doesn't happen always.

It takes perseverance to turn weaknesses into strength. It takes a lot of guts to fight alone. There are many instances when a child born with any disability has proven everybody wrong on the assumption that he won't be able to achieve anything. Take this example. A child was being born with crippled legs. To be able to walk on his feet was a distant dream, let alone to run. Doctors had given up all the hopes for the child. But his mother was not willing to lose her faith. She would teach him little by little. She would make him practice all the exercises in the gentlest possible ways. To the surprise of many people the boy was able to stand on his own feet. He was able to run. He even secured a place in the Paralympics games.

Take this example. A girl was born with mental retardation added to some other ailments. Doctors had given up every hope of the girl's future as an adult. Her parents didn't budge. They put in all their efforts into making the child speak, walk, and talk on her own. The little things that are easy for an average child would prove too hard for the girl. But the parents were hopeful. Their efforts paid off. Though slow on the road to the progress, the girl began to do everything on her own. The consistent efforts led the girl to participate in the national swimming championship in the Paralympics. The girl attended and won a silver medal in the competition.

Every child is special, and every life is sacred.

# *HOW PEOPLE JUDGE YOUR PAST*

## The guilt trap

A parachute jumper had a near-death experience in the past. As a result, he started to avoid the particular sport. Fear only ends at the place, it began first. The jumper needs to re-experience the incident in order to overcome the horrific experience. Once you learn to embrace the learning, it sets you free. Unless you don't forgive yourselves, how will you move on? Just because you did a car accident in the past doesn't mean you should abstain from driving. A series of failed relationships in the past shouldn't stop you from seeking new relationships.

A drug smuggler doesn't want to do smuggling all his life. A murderer doesn't want to be a killer all his life. Again, because you stole something in the past doesn't mean that you are a thief for the rest of your life. The greatest thing you can learn from the past is to embrace the past mistake, to learn the lessons, and to forgive yourself. Often, we cling to our past mistakes so tight that we miss to learn the lessons. We focus more on the errors. Most importantly we forget to forgive ourselves. We don't grow ourselves and not let others grow as well. Often, we miss the valuable learning of life.

Take this example. A young woman had been molested by someone very close to her. She had never thought in her wildest dream that it could happen to her. As a result, she began to avoid all the men. She began to look at every man with suspicion. Does avoiding men help her overcome the emotional trauma? The only way to overcome the pain is to talk about it. She must see it for herself that the culprit gets punished.

Labeling all the men as bad is not okay.

Take another example. X was trying to change the lane on a highway. There were a lot of other people driving on the wrong side of the track. Suddenly another car cut across the lane from the wrong side of the track and collided. In an attempt to put on the brakes, X accidently hit the second car. The second car went off the road uncontrollably. Nobody can ever predict what could go wrong on a highway. It happened in a fraction of second. The driver of the second car got hit in the collision and died on the spot. X was not at his fault. Still, he had to suffer the consequences; he was being sentenced to jail for obviously no fault of his. He felt humiliated in his own eyes. The person hasn't touched the car since the accident. Would it serve him any purpose? Do you think that the driver should begin to drive again?

## Look within first

A deep introspection within can answer many questions. Making mistakes is human. But care should be taken not to repeat the same error. Nothing changes you like the willingness to change. Think of the family and children of a murderer or a fraud. Their whole life goes in proving that they are not akin to the murderer or the fraud. They become the object of scrutiny everywhere. They have to pay the price despite being innocent.

Our life impacts so many other lives. If you are looked down upon because of your poor background, you shouldn't feel ashamed of it. In fact, many great people had humble beginnings. You were a poor person in the past; it doesn't mean that you cannot dream of being rich. You were an immoral person in the past; it doesn't mean that you cannot be a moral person today. Again, if you had a series of failed relationships in the past; it doesn't mean that you would be having failed relationships the whole life. Whether it was a past mistake, a wrong doing, or a poor beginning, you can always start again. All of us had a past, but it shouldn't stop us from growing. People are going to judge. Embrace your past mistakes. Don't run away from them. Learn from them.

## Embrace your past

Some people have the habit of running away from their past. No amount of running away from the past would help. If running away from the problem helped, it would have helped the millions of people who have the habit of running away from their past.

*When any amount of running away doesn't help; learn the ways to deal with the situation.*

You killed someone in an accident in the past. No amount of running away helps. Though unintentionally, you had killed someone. Try to reach out to the deceased's family members. Try to help them in any possible way – emotionally, spiritually, or monetarily. It will bring you more peace than running away. The only way to peace is to accept your responsibilities.

The thing is, if you learn from your past mistakes, you can move forward toward a new life. No matter what you did in the past, you can always begin again. You had a trouble in having a good start in the beginning of a car race; it doesn't mean that you would end up finishing the last. The past unresolved emotions would reoccur on a frequent basis if left unattended.

Unless you have a deep introspection of your life, you will remain stuck in your past. We never have the time to understand why the past is still alive. Unless the past emotions are fully resolved, we cannot find the way to a new life. The only way to prevent the past from reoccurring is to understand it. The past will continue to interfere with our present when we don't embrace the past mistakes.

## Is this your story?

A man was destitute. He had no food, no water, and no money. If this was not enough, he had an ailing mother, a wife, and three small children. Out of desperation to do something the young man thought of breaking into a bank and stealing some money. The destined day came. He waited. The predetermined time arrived. Fate was also favoring him. The only watchman of the bank fell asleep. Slowly the man took the keys that were kept beneath the watchman and entered the bank.

The area in which the bank was situated was small with a limited number of people. The area was not well developed. The security system of the bank was too easy to break in. The man did the same. He quickly collected the money in the small bag that he had brought from the home. The man could have collected a lot of money, but he didn't. He was needy and not greedy. He collected only a handful of money in the bag and began to flee. As he was about to reach the door of the bank, the watchman came in. The watchman had no weapon but had informed the police. The man froze. Time stood standstill. The police came and arrested the man. The police confiscated all the money from the man and handed it back to the bank.

Had the man been not so needy, would he have attempted to steal?

*The second part.*

The man is freed after spending seven years in jail. The real identity crisis begins now. People don't recognize him. Now, he is known as a prison convict who was caught stealing. He was not the only one to suffer; his family had their share of suffering. Like the man, the family had now become the family of a jail convict. Wherever they went, their identity went along with them.

The real problem began when the man actually went out to seek some job. Everywhere he was rejected. His past followed him wherever he went. Life had again brought him on to the situation; he was seven years ago. He was helpless, jobless, and without any provisions. If people had accepted him as they would have done in case of their beloved ones, the whole story would have been different. The question is not whether stealing is a good or bad. Stealing is certainly wrong.

Why we do not give one chance to a person who wants to rectify his mistakes?

## Heal the past

Remember the time you got wounded and it began bleeding. What did you do? Did you leave the wound as it is? The wound would remain as it is; until you heal the wound with the help of proper medicine. Unless the past life issues and the unresolved emotions are resolved completely, the past traumas and the unresolved emotions from the past keep on lingering over. Unless you are healed completely, you cannot move ahead in your life. A complete healing cannot be done. You cannot carry the burden of your past for the whole life. Isn't it?

To move on, you need to unburden yourselves. Forgiving those who have caused you the pain is the only way. Eventually, it's your karmas that lead to downfall. You got to let go of the past. You have to free yourself of the pain. In other words, you have to detach yourselves from the painful past. Detachment is a concept in Buddhism. Detachment doesn't mean that you have to passively sit and see the things happening. Detachment means that you are detaching yourself from the source of pain. Whether it's the pain from the past or a hurtful person, forgiving is always the best solution.

*When someone kept you hungrily purposefully for days together, either of the two things will happen; you will be keeping someone else hungry in revenge, or you will be feeding in compassion for others.*

No matter how difficult the past, you can always move ahead in life. You can break free from the shackles of the past. Sometimes, it's the pain from the past that prevents us from moving ahead in life. Unless you are completely free of the grudges of the past, you cannot move forward in life. The burden of the past keeps lingering over. We hold on to the pain of the past too rigidly. The past prevents us from living our present. The past continues to haunt unless you embrace it fully. No amount of running away from the past ever helps. Making mistakes is human. Everybody makes mistakes, but how you learn your lessons is your part. Nobody else can help you. Accept your past mistakes, learn the lessons, forgive yourself, and move forward in life.

## Things change, so do people

*No matter how hard the past, you can always begin new. – The Buddha.*

It doesn't matter what you were in the past. What is important is what you are today. Whether you were a scoundrel, an addict, or a fraud, it doesn't matter, if you are a good person today. What is important is the effort you are putting to change yourself. A troubled past can turn into a bright present. Again, an imperfect present can turn into a bright future. You never know how a person in the past would turn into an entirely different person today.

An inconsiderate person in the past may become a compassionate person today. A cruel person in the past may become a kind person today. Likewise, a bad guy may become a good one. But, we never accept the change. We cling to our past perceptions. People judge by your past. They don't give you a chance to change. If you were a fraud twenty years back, it doesn't mean you will be a fraud for your whole life. God never condemns anyone. He never goes by the people's perception. God readily forgives.

We don't forgive ourselves.

A person had murdered someone. He was sentenced to fourteen years of incarceration. Later, he was set free. He had a tough time gaining social acceptance. His self-esteem suffered. He tried to appear for the interviews but everywhere he was rejected. His dubious past came as a block. There was no one to help him. Out of frustration, he ended his life. Was ending the life the only solution?

## How do you judge this?

A person was a murderer in the past. Today he is a decent man earning a decent livelihood. The stigma of the past continues to haunt even today. The family has to suffer too. No matter where they go, no matter what they do, the past is still alive. Whether it's the children admission to the school, an opening of a bank account, or the enrollment in the government register, and no matter what the circumstances are, the ghost of the past continues to haunt, not only to the man but to his family as well. The family despite being innocent has to share the burden of the suffering due to the man's past. The painful thing about the past is; it affects not only you but also to the people around you. The past can have a profound effect on you. You go on reliving the past over and over again.

Like a reel of a film, we consciously or unconsciously keep on rewinding the past. Like a woman who had been molested in the past continues to experience the horrifying experience till date. What's the point of being stuck in the past? Unless the past gets healed, the future cannot be hale and hearty.

It doesn't matter that you are in a respectable position today; the fact that you were born out of the wedlock continues to haunt you. It is clearly evident that sometimes we have to suffer even after no fault of ours. Sometimes it is tough to escape the past. People like to judge everything. When it comes to judging your past, they do it even harder. Like your present life, every aspect of your past is scrutinized as well. Past mistakes are not forgiven. In the end, no amount of people-pleasing, donating a huge amount of money to the charity, or running away from the past, can help you escape the hook off the painful past. No matter how many times you have donated a huge amount of money in charity; people would still remember that your father was a drug smuggler of yesteryears.

No matter how successful you are today, the past lingers on.

## You cannot escape your past

Everyone wants to run away from their past. A wealthy person intent on showing his riches today had the past full of poverty. A scholar intent on proving his intelligence today had the past of being labeled as foolish. Again, an extremely health conscious person today was a fat person in the past.

No matter where you go, your past follows. You might be a respectable person today, but people don't forget the fact that you had killed someone in the past. No amount of donating money today washes the wrong impression of yesterday. Your whole life goes into proving people that whatever the past had been, but today you are a good human being. You may be a successful businessman today; people still remember the fact that you were a fraud and a convict in the past. Past mistakes are not forgiven easily.

## Is this your story?

A person is a priest in the temple. Today he seems to be peaceful and unperturbed with the daily chaos of the life. He gives correct advice to anyone who seeks his guidance. People do not know his past story, but it agitates him. His previous story continues to haunt him even today. The priest was a child then. He was being raised by his mother alone in the hilly area near a forest. The house was in complete solitude with the rest of the city. It was easy for anyone to break in the house as the mother and son were easy targets. On that unfortunate day, few men entered the priest's house. The thieves were looking for the mother's ornaments and some other valuables.

After looting all the valuables, the thieves began misbehaving with the priest's mother. In the desperation to save his mother, the child hit one of the thieves. The person died on the spot. Though the other men fled away, and the priest's mother was saved, the incident left an indelible impression on the priest's mind. Wherever he goes, his past follows. Whether people know about your past or not, the pain from the past continues to remain locked within. It's like being able to run from everyone else, but not being able to run away from yourself. Though what happened was unintentional, still, the priest holds himself solely responsible for the incident. The past is still alive for the priest.

## Is this your story?

There were two convicts in the jail. Both of them were being held for the same guilt – murder.

However, there was a difference. For the sake of simplicity let's name the first person as X, who didn't commit the murder. Someone had cunningly put the charges of murder on him. X got punished for no fault of his. He always remained full of anger, guilt, and resentment. All the time spent in the jail went in blaming that person, and thinking that the world is full of wrong people. He thought, *"I hate living in this world. Where was god, when all this was happening to me? He could have saved me?"* The whole tenure of fourteen years went in this way, blaming himself and cursing others.

As soon as X was being released from the jail, he tried hard to find the person who had deceitfully put him into the prison. On finding the person, X killed him in a fit of rage. All the fourteen years of resent that got built up during the jail had to come out, and it came, but in the negative way. Though X was innocent earlier, but now he was a murderer.

*Think about it.* The point is not whether X was right or wrong.

By taking the law in his own hands, now he was as guilty as the real murderer. Fourteen years of jail term could be utilized into deep introspection of things. Instead, he channelized all his energy into seeking revenge. Fourteen years spent in the jail are enough to change you; you could become what you never were. But in this case, the contrary happened. X was again sentenced to a fresh jail term of fourteen years.

## The second part

The second person who was convicted for murder had turned the story differently. Initially, he was resentful. Later, he decided that if he has to spend his fourteen years in the jail, why not utilize the time into something useful? He began volunteering as a teacher for the other inmates in the jail. He began teaching others.

As his whole energy was directed into something new and useful, the dark chapters of the past went back to the past. On the destined day, the man was released from the jail. The good work and the goodwill accumulated during the bad days in the jail had helped him become a better man. *It is said that things change, when you change.* It was going to be true in this case. Thanks to his ability to work hard, he immediately got a job within few days after being released from the jail. Soon after he got settled and today is a proud father of three lovely kids. What a happy ending to a poor beginning. Isn't it?

## How would you judge this?

A drug smuggler doesn't want to continue smuggling all his life. A murderer doesn't want to be a killer his whole life. In fact, it's a good thing that a drug smuggler doesn't want to remain a smuggler his entire life. A murderer doesn't want to remain a killer his whole life. In other words, everybody wants to escape from the prison of the past. People want to be a totally different person than they were in the past. Just because you were a murderer in the past, it doesn't mean that you cannot be a right person today. But, people will try to make sure you keep recalling the incident.

In fact, it's a good thing that people want to transform their present. If you had a poor past, then you must have a desire to get rid of poverty and become rich. Unless you don't want to leave your poor past behind, how could anyone help you? In other words, if you have a strong desire to change your past life, only then you will be able to transform your present. An immoral person in the past is now an extremely righteous person. A smuggler of yesteryears is now a religious person. Again, a struggling actor who had to do the odd jobs in the past is now a well-established artist. You were a drug addict in the past; this doesn't mean that you cannot be a good human being today. But, escaping the past is not always easy.

It is because of our own fear and unwillingness to forgive ourselves; we are locked forever in the past. Unless you are willing to forgive yourself, you would remain stuck in the past. People go on punishing themselves many times for the mistake they did once. When it comes to forgiving others, most people readily forgive. When it comes to forgiving themselves, people do not readily forgive. In other words, forgiving others is easy while forgiving yourself is not. We go on hurting ourselves for years together.

You made a mistake like everybody else; and you should have readily forgiven yourself. In the process of forgiving others, you tend to forget that you were the most hurt in the process. People hurt you and go away. You kept hurting yourself for years together. It was you who kept holding on to the pain for so many years. In other words, you have hurt yourself the most. The one who needs to be immediately forgiven is you. Everyone makes mistakes. After all, it's human to make mistakes.

Unintentionally, we hurt ourselves in such a way that even our worst enemy would also not hurt. Sometimes we can get extremely cruel with ourselves. We keep holding on to the pain and the resentment for years together. The pain has to go somewhere; either you keep it within and let it turn into a bigger wound, or you burst it out on to others. The pain within will eventually leads to a major illness. Again, the pain which is vented out to others would hurt them.

Later, we justify ourselves saying that it's because people caused us pain, so, we, in turn caused pain to them. It is like; I am going to cheat on somebody because someone else cheated on me. Is it justified that I am free to make fun of someone because somebody else made fun of me? In the end, the person who hurt you the most was none other than you. Before you forgive anybody else, forgive yourself, because you were the one who was hurt the most. The hurt and the resentment, we had experienced in the past has to be vented out through a proper channel. The pain that we kept locked for years within us has to be freed and released. Forgiving is the best way. It takes nothing to forgive. It would release all the bitterness from within in a gentle way. Forgiving is the best way to break off the shackles of the past and move ahead in life.

# *HOW PEOPLE JUDGE YOUR APPEARANCE*

## Looks can be deceptive

*You are fat.*
*You are tall.*
*You are dull.*
*You are a good-for-nothing.*

Whether it's the person's way of eating, dressing, or the speaking style, we can never predict anything accurately if we draw conclusions from the surface. A person is fat and tends to overeat. We immediately label him as fatty and begin to judge that he shouldn't be eating so much of food. We even label the person as careless and irresponsible towards oneself. When we look more deeply, we understand that out of loneliness and depression the person overeats.

Behind every story, there is another story. We never know the whole thing. To judge a person entirely upon his external appearances is to judge the depth of a river. It's highly unpredictable. We mistake a cruel hearted person for a kind hearted. We get highly impressed because of his nice way of talking. 'A good man may be under a poor coat,' goes the Scottish saying.

Too much emphasis is laid for the external appearance. A poor person need not necessarily be a thief. But, when we find that something has been stolen from our house, we think that the culprit has to be the poor housemaid. Stealing has got nothing to do with poverty. Stealing has to do more with greed. In fact, there are cases where people from well-to-do family have been caught stealing. It's only when we try to see the whole picture, the whole story appears.

A seemingly kind person attends the religious meetings regularly. He is always soft-spoken and gives a lot of money in charity. He may not be the same inside. In fact, when the person is accused of assaulting his maid, we get astonished as it seems unbelievable. This truth is contrary to what it appeared on the surface.

Similarly, a seemingly meek person is accused of assaulting his fellow mates. When we hear something like this, we find it hard to believe that a humble person can also attack. We surely are on the wrong track, when we don't take the whole picture into account. If we are already pre-occupied with our own assumptions, how will we be able to find out the truth? Without considering the larger picture, one cannot find out the hidden truth.

If a school has large building and charges a hefty fee, we immediately jump to the conclusion that the school teaches well. If a hospital is expensive and charges substantial bills, we quickly jump to the conclusion that the hospital might be good, otherwise, why a hospital would charge so much of fees? Again, if a restaurant digs deeply into our pocket; we think the food might be good. But, in actual there is no direct link between the expensive bills and the quality of food, the hefty fees and the quality teaching, and the heavy medical bills and the good medical care. Predictions are predictions. It may or may not be true.

*Your best judge is you.*

A person wearing expensive clothes doesn't necessarily mean that he has to be a good person. The outward appearances can be cleverly concealed; the real person cannot be. Likewise, a seemingly healthy person might actually be unhealthy from inside. Judgments based upon the outer appearances alone may not be true. Whether it's a relationship, individuals, or situations, things are not always as they appear to be. The real truth may be in total contrast to the visible truth. Without taking into account the whole picture, one should never jump to the conclusions.

A woman would be rude to everyone. When asked something, she would never give a proper reply. Later, it comes that she had been hurt many times, and if this was not enough, she had lost her only son in an accident. She had become paranoid. So, she began to doubt everything and everyone. Things are not always as they appear on the surface. We should not jump to conclusions without taking everything into consideration.

## How you judge this?

1) *Girls wearing makeup are less moral than the girls abstaining makeup.*
   *It's not true. A girl may be wearing makeup because of her profession demands or because she is fond of it. The external appearances do not define morality.*

2) *A woman is at fault if she is divorced.*
   *It's not true. Anybody can be at fault when it comes to divorce. There are a lot of other reasons too. Gender has got nothing to do with the divorce.*

3) *A student who wears spectacles is very studious.*
   *It's not true. A student may be wearing spectacles due to his poor eye-sight or as a part of his style statement.*

*4) A single man cannot raise children alone.*
*It's not true. There are no evidences that a man cannot raise children single-handily. In fact, many single fathers taking good care of their children.*

## How would you judge this?

We cannot stop ourselves from judging. We inspect everything. Right from the small details, to the larger picture, we carefully see every detail. Whether it's a person's appearance, the body language, the accent, or the behavior, the scrutiny goes on. We are always on a vigil. But the depth of an ocean cannot be found by merely looking at it. We give too much importance to the outer appearances. The more emphasis on the outward appearance, the more we distance ourselves from the greater truth. And opinion solely based upon a person's outward appearance can be misleading.

We see a person in police uniform and immediately begin obeying his orders. We never pause to think that why a police officer would demand our gold ornaments. The officer asked us to hand over the ornaments for keeping safely with him, and we immediately began obeying the orders without giving any second thought. The whole story is dubious in the first place itself; we never give a second thought to such things.

We see a salesman dressed in a well-fitting suit, speaking English fluently in an American accent, and is extremely confident. We literally jump to accept his offer to buy a rare piece of antique, only to regret it later. We later find out the antique to be a fake one. Again, what made us pay a huge amount of money for buying the antique? The answer is simple, the appearance. We thought that a person in the expensive suit has to be rich and decent. We thought that he could never deceive. When it comes to deceiving, anyone can deceive. It's because of the tendency to give too much of importance to the external appearances of things, we get lost in the middle itself. We never fully understand the deeper truth. Deceiving can't be reserved for the poor alone.

The reason why a placebo works so effectively is due to our tendency to give too much importance to the outer appearances. In fact, a placebo is not a medicine in the first place. The patient takes the placebo not knowing that it is not a medicine, and surprisingly gets healthy too. Isn't it strange that how a person is given a placebo and surprisingly the patient gets well too? Studies have confirmed that placebo actually works. This proves that how important are the external appearances to us. In fact, it's because of the patient's own belief that helps us overcome the illness and become healthy again.

Take this example. There are two doctors. Both are equally qualified and capable. But one doctor is practices in a relatively small clinic and charges less fees. The other doctor practices in an expensive multi-storied building and charges heavily. Though both the doctors are equally qualified, we only want to be treated by the second doctor? Why? It's strange that how expensive a hospital is a matter of concern. Is there a guarantee that a posh hospital would treat a patient more effectively? In fact, there is no connection between a big hospital and getting healthier.

Labels like good or bad, fat or thin, mediocre or genius, and rich or poor are given. We do not see the whole picture. But, we immediately jump to the conclusions. It is only when you can see the deeper truth; you can understand so many things better. Again, the stereotypes are the most difficult to tackle. People assume things according to their experiences and then label people according to their limited beliefs.

Consider this example. There are two men in the room. The first man is rich and is nicely dressed in a well-fitted suit; the second man is dressed shoddily and is a relatively poor. A woman accuses of being molested in the room. What's our reaction? Without even blinking our eye, we immediately jump to the conclusion that the shoddily dressed person might have done something wrong with the woman. Why? Even without knowing the whole story, how can we conclude that the shoddily dressed person might have done something? Is there any logic in saying that a person in a well-fitted suit cannot be a molester? Why a shoddily dressed poor person has to be the molester? What has the lust got to do with being poor or rich? Lust only wants to get fulfilled. *A man in a well stitched suit may or may not be a gentleman.* Based on the outer appearances of a person, we quickly judge a good looking person to be a gentleman. Everything that appears to be true may not be always true.

Take this example. A relatively wealthy woman accuses her poor maid of stealing. What is our first reaction? We immediately jump to the conclusion that the maid might be a thief. Just because a woman is poor and is dressed in rags; it doesn't mean that she has to be the thief. But, we think that a poor person has to be a thief and a rich person cannot steal. Is there any basis for such assumptions? Rich people can also commit stealing.

Consider this example. When we come to know that a child has been accused of shop-lifting in the shop. What's our first reaction? We immediately pick the poorest of all the children present in the shop and then start strip-searching the kids. And the result? We find a comparatively rich kid had stolen the stuff. Shocking! Isn't it? We think that a rich person with good etiquettes is enough for being content. In fact, you can be rich but still be greedy; while you can be poor and still be content. What has greed got to do with poverty or affluence? Being greedy is a state of mind. Based on our experiences we put labels on people. We judge people on their external appearances.

Whether it's a job interview, lending money to someone, or a marriage proposal, we only get to know the person for a short time. In such a short lifespan of time, we have to decide many things. You meet a person and immediately decide to marry him or her. A five minutes judgment can cost dearly sometimes. If you judge someone based entirely upon their external appearances alone, there are chances that you would be making the greatest mistake of your life.

# *HOW PEOPLE JUDGE YOUR WEIGHT*

## You can't escape being judged

People often judge. Weight is one of the parameters. Whether you are skinny or fat, you are going to be scrutinized by people. A thin person is judged for not eating enough. A fat person is judged for not exercising enough. If we apply our compassion towards a person's eating habits, we can clearly understand many things. A neutral perspective towards the people's food diet reveals a lot of things. People are ever-ready to advice you. *Try this. Try that. Avoid this. Avoid doing that.*

It's not that all advices are ill-intentioned. But even a well-intentioned advice hurts sometimes. Like other issues, weight is a highly personal concept. When I accept myself, the way I am, it doesn't matter what people have to say. No matter what you eat and how much you exercise, you would be judged. Why bother being judged? You cannot escape being judged in either way.

## Your body as a projection of yourself

We have an ideal view of the ideal body weight for the different professions. Ideally, a gym instructor should have an athletic body with a strong muscular shape. The gym trainer should matchup to our expectations by looking fit enough. When we come across a gym instructor who is obese and has a tired look, what do we think? Would we like to get trained in that particular gym? What opinions do we form about the gym instructor? We begin to think that if a person himself can't keep his own body in a fit condition, how he will be able to keep the others fit and healthy.

To instill an idea of a healthy body in others, you have to project it through yourself first. It's like; I am telling others how to be healthy even though I weigh around too much. No one is going to take it seriously. Isn't it? There are certain professions which require a proper projection of its professionals. The problem lies in the way the truth is being interpreted. A wrong interpretation leads to the wrong results.

Likewise, what do we think when we go to a doctor for a treatment? If a doctor himself is unhealthy, how will he treat his patients? Isn't it right? A doctor with a healthy body will instill a sense of confidence in the patients. Some people would argue that what has the weight factor got to do with the better treatment of the patients? As a leader in any field, you are the role-models for the people. If a doctor himself looks dull, tired, obese and unhealthy, what message does it convey to the patients?

Likewise, if a gym instructor himself is fat, tired, or unhealthy, what message does it pass on to the people around him? There are certain professions which require that the body size and the health should be taken very seriously. Whether it's the medical profession, the sport profession, the modeling field, or the hospitality sector, there are certain professions where you have to project the profession through a body that fits into the mold of the ideal body weight. A profession is best projected through its professionals.

## Your best judge is you

In fact, more emphasis should be given on health rather on the appearances. Many fat people are as healthy as anybody else. To the contrary, there are many size-zero people who score low on the health parameters. No matter what people say about you weight, it's for you to decide what is right for you. In the end, what matters is how happy you are with yourself. There are some professions like modeling and acting where having well-toned body is a must. You have to fit into a certain body frame. Still, it's your choice how you like to project it through yourself. You like it or hate it; you cannot avoid the already existing norm in these professions.

When I am happy with the way I look, I would be more authentic in representing myself. It is only when I am not happy; I would be hiding myself. Everything comes down to only one thing, when I am happy with myself, nobody else can make me feel inferior. Weight is a highly personal concept. It has more to do with the inner thoughts. Weight has nothing to do with the happiness. You can be as happy as you make your mind to be. *There is no need to fit into others mold.* You are your best judge to decide what's good for you and what is not.

Whether it's for food, clothes, or career, nobody else can judge for you. You are the best judge. Whether it's the profession's demand to stay fit and healthy or a personal choice, it's all up to you to take the decisions. You should decide what lies in your best interest. The more we understand and respect our body, the happier we become. Nothing should be done against the body. The body has its own intelligence. The body knows exactly how much of fat should be stored for the future use and how much of fat should be utilized for the daily purpose. Any attempt to change the delicate balance of hormones or metabolism may prove harmful. Whether you are fat, thin, or skinny, learn to embrace it. Rejoice the fact that you are alive. Love yourself.

## Empathic judging

When we see a woman eating too much of food, we immediately conclude that she is overweight person and she needs to lose her weight. We don't take the pain to actually find out the whole story. On knowing the woman further it comes that she had been divorced from her husband. She was finding it tough to face the challenges of life. So, it took a toll on her health. You may call her a victim of emotional eating. Often, we miss the deeper truths of the life by looking on the surface.

Take this example. We see a boy resorting to violent measures in the school and throwing tantrums. Everybody quickly mistakes him for a spoiled brat. But, the inside story was in total contrast to the surface one. The boy had an abusive father who would always resort to the violent measures. His poor mother could do nothing but to endure it. The boy's behavior changed drastically because of this problem. To understand human emotions, we have to become empathetic. You cannot be robotic and yet able to comprehend human emotions. By a simple observation, we can make out that a person is in trouble and needs help.

If we see a person hungry, and we still choose to pass by, what does it mean? If we see a person shivering terribly in the cold, and if we decide to pass by, what does it mean? Again, if we see a person dying of thirst, and if we choose to ignore his pleas to provide him water, what does it mean? Why can't the pain in somebody, evoke empathy in us? Unless we change the way we look at things, we won't be able to see the real person.

A person is too apologetic even after no fault of his. We fail to understand that the individual is suffering from low self-esteem.

We miss the greater truth by missing the larger picture. Likewise, a person trying too hard to achieve perfectionism is a terribly insecure person. Failing to understand why a person behaves in a certain way leads to the wrong conclusions. Be compassionate. It helps to solve many problems.

# *HOW PEOPLE JUDGE OTHERS RELIGION*

*Never hurt any living being. This is the true religion. -The Buddha*

From time to time great souls like Christ, Muhammad, Buddha have descended on earth and taught us peace, love, and brotherhood. But, we forget their lessons and begin fighting with each other in the name of religion. No religion has ever taught hatred, ill-will, and enmity. Still, we fight in the name of religion. There comes a time when we get fanatical about our religion, ideas, views, verdicts and judgments. We begin to see the supposedly good things entirely in our religion and all the evil things entirely in the others' religion.

We live in a family. We learn many things from the people around us, the society in general, and the community in larger. Our beliefs, attitudes, and verdicts are significantly shaped by these factors. In other words, our surroundings have a profound impact on our minds. Again, it's natural that we would absorb the harmful teachings from our surroundings. We believe those teachings to be true. It is natural that everyone else would be thinking in the same way. Everyone believes their own religious teachings to be true. We never feel the need to question these beliefs. Over a period, these ideas become rigid in our minds. Often, these beliefs are hard to change and difficult to deal. A point comes when we block our growth. We don't let others grow as well. We create obstacles in their way. Often, we get too intent on proving to others that our religion is the best. The atmosphere gets tensed, people fight with each other, and many precious lives are lost, unnecessarily in the name of religion. Every religion has taught us to choose peace over war, love over hatred, and brotherhood over enmity. Still, we fight with each other and try to pull one another down.

## My religion, their religion

Are you from our religion too? I have heard people asking this question during their conversation. I never really understood what the term *ours* mean? We feel instantly connected to somebody when they are from our religion. We immediately feel a sense of deep connection of brotherhood. But, when somebody is of a faith different from ours, we don't feel the same for them. I have failed to understand what does the term *'our religion'* means? Don't all religion teach us to love each other despite the differences? Isn't humanity the greatest of all the religion? It's because of the distinction of *ours* and *theirs;* the world has seen so many wars.

All the wars have been fought to prove whose religion is superior of all? To prove that our religion is best, we have fought many wars, many times. It's strange that we fight first, to have peace. No religion in the world has taught us to fight in name of god. But, we still fight. When hatred precedes over love, enmity precedes over brotherhood, and revenge precedes over forgiveness, the world becomes a scary place to live. Religion brings a sense of togetherness. Religion brings the whole world together, and strangely enough the same religion can also be used to divide us as well. We are ever ready to prove that our religion is the best of all.

Religion brings peace. Our own belief brings us hatred, enmity, and bitterness. The problem doesn't lie with the religion; the actual problem lies in the way the truth is being interpreted. We modify the teachings of our religion and then apply it. No religion has taught hatred or enmity, but we do. The problem lies in the wrong interpretation of religion. No religion has ever taught of killing the innocent. Some people think that god would be pleased with the killing of innocent people and would reward a place in the heaven. This is absolutely wrong.

We modify the teachings of religion for ourselves, and we teach others to do the same.

*If religion can't bring us peace, then it shouldn't be a source of bringing violence either.*

## The real problem begins here

We get an early impression that our way of doing things, thinking, and understanding things are the best like no other. We forget that others might also be thinking in the same way. The real clash begins here. Each one of us is fighting to prove that their ideologies are the best. No one is actually interested in following the religion's teachings themselves. People are more interested in teaching about their own viewpoint rather than empathically listening to others. The actual problem arises here.

Each one of us is more interested in preaching others. Nobody is actually willing to listen. Everybody is busy proving that their religion is the best. People are more interested in proving their religion is the best. A word becomes empty without action. We may read a lot of holy books, what is the use of the knowledge, if we don't follow the teachings? We know too much, but we understand too little. Again, if something is the best, why need to prove it? Why do we need to prove it? The sun doesn't go around proving that it's the sun. Again, the moon doesn't go around proving that it's the moon. It's clearly evident that no forces of nature choose to waste its energy in proving itself. Instead of wasting the precious time and energy into proving whose religion is best, we can channelize all our valuable energies into making a better world. Wisdom is wisdom, no matter the source. The source of wisdom is immaterial. Can't we put aside our differences and walk together in peace? Is the source of knowledge more important than the actual knowledge itself?

## Distorted truth

Teaching the right things in the right way is a big responsibility. Truth should be interpreted in its original context; nothing should be added nor should anything be subtracted. A surface observation gives a surface truth. A profound observation gives the deeper truths of life. Wisdom is valuable when it's retained in the original structure. To the contrary, wisdom is invaluable when it's distorted.

*Truth, when distorted is no longer the truth, it becomes distorted truth.*

God created the world hoping that we would live with peace, love, and forgiveness. But, we have created an entirely different world by creating rivalry, bitterness, humility, hatred, and divisions. No religion intends to bring divisions or hatred among people. If we are a loyal follower of our respective religion, we have to practice the virtues taught in the holy books. Likewise, we can destroy the world with our hateful thoughts or make the world a beautiful place to live. No great soul has ever taught us to spread hatred and violence, but we do.

## Apply your own wisdom

There are many contradictory things in regards to different religions. Whether it's the way of thinking, the way of doing things, the food habits, the clothes, the way of earning livelihood, or any another aspect, every religion has contradicting theories. Often, people go on fighting with each other to prove that their way of thinking is the best. Take this example. One religion allows having meat while the other religion tells to avoid meat. In one religion there are certain days which are considered as sacred. To the contrary, a completely different set of days may be considered as sacred in the other religion. In some religion the dead are cremated while the dead are buried in the other.

In the end, it's the love, inner peace, and calmness that matter the most to the humanity. No matter what the religion, peace is the last search. Every person should pause a while and check himself whether he is on the right track. We see and hear many things that may not be actually true. Often, we blindly accept these things without questioning the credibility of the source. If someone is doing a certain thing in a particular way, we follow the same way of doing things without thinking of the consequences. Often, it's the blind faith that takes us to nowhere. We end up getting lost. Sometimes we need to question the way of doing things? Why are we blindly following others? Why are we not living with honesty? Where are we leading ourselves?

It's crucial for each one of us to find out whether our way of thinking and doing things are correct? We would be teaching our children, what we had been taught by our parents. Again, our children would be teaching the same things to their next generation. Nobody feels the need to question these beliefs. It is where the major problem exists. There is nothing wrong in teaching the right things; the problems lie in the incorrect interpretation.

Often, we modify the truth according to our needs and convenience. If we don't introspect ourselves now, it will prove to be too late for the next generations. We have been teaching our children, what our previous generations taught us. Again, if there was something wrong in the teaching, we would be unknowingly handing them over to our further generations. Think for a while; is it the correct thing to do? It's always better to teach the right things in the right way. We never give poisoned food to our children, then why do we poison their innocent minds with hateful thoughts?

Can't we teach love, peace, humility, forgiveness, and brotherhood to our children?

## Every religion teaches forgiveness

If you want to win over each other, the only way to win is through love. Hate cannot be won by hate. Enmity cannot be won by enmity. Likewise, violence cannot be won by violence. Killing in revenge would lead to even more bloodshed. Gandhi's saying holds a high relevance in this context; an eye for eye ends up making the whole world blind. An eye for eye would end up making the world a scary place to live. A turbulent thought leads to troubled times. Your inner turmoil is going to affect you, your family, the society, and the whole world in the end.

Your thoughts, opinions, views, and judgments immensely affect others in a profound way. What we do when somebody hurt us? We immediately jump in to take revenge. Isn't it? We think ourselves to be a great believer of our religion, but what happens when we get hurt by others? Why don't we practice forgiveness like the great souls taught us? Why is that we believe in the religion, but do not follow the teachings ourselves?

There is a story in the Bible where Jesus Christ forgave the soldiers who crucified him. "Father, forgive them, for they know not what they are doing," said Jesus Christ. Can't we do the same? Can't we forgive our enemies easily without any traces of enmity and bitterness left inside? Many different paths lead us to the supreme god. It's the reaching to the final destination matters.

We all are on a journey called life. Each individual according to his or her capacity is on the road to the self-evolution. One person would be trying to reach the end destination by the cycle, the other by car, and some would be trying to reach the end destination by airplane. Whether you choose to reach the path by road, by air, or by sea hardly matter. The mode of the transport is immaterial. The same holds true for all of us. In the end, it's reaching the destination matters. Any mode of transport is good; till it helps you reach the final destination. Likewise any religion is good; till it helps you bond with god.

# *HOW PEOPLE JUDGE YOUR PROFESSION*

## Have a thought

When you are working for 6-8 hours daily, it adds up to 180 hours a month, and finally it adds up to 2160 hours a year, it's imperative that you derive inner satisfaction and pleasure when you are spending 2160 hours of your life into something,

*Yes, I am a worker in that bakery.*
*I don't find my job fulfilling.*
*My job brings me shame.*
*I want to quit but can't.*

If you are a cobbler and you don't like the job to mend the shoes? Again, if you are a waiter and you don't like to serve your customers? Likewise, if a person is a gym instructor and he doesn't likes the profession itself? If your work is not energizing you, it shouldn't drain you either. When you are putting in so much of energy into something, you should feel energetic and not drained at the end of the day. Even if you are able to draw huge money by literally draining yourselves into work; in the end, it is you who would suffer the most. Your health, mind, body, and the soul will have to suffer. Work is not the source of earning money alone. It should be a source of joy, happiness, faith, cooperation, and communication.

## The dignity of labor

You used to clean dishes for livelihood. Somebody suggests you a better place with a better salary. However well-intentioned the advice, it hurts inside. Why?

Why you feel ashamed of your job? Some people have grudges that they don't find their jobs fulfilling. Still they have are left with no other option but to continue. Working without joy is like eating slow poison. It is killing you from within. If you have no other option left, but to continue with your job, then what to do? You have to accept the fact that your job is your source of livelihood. When you are deriving your livelihood from work, you should respect it as well. What's the point in continuing the job when you don't love it?

*If your work is not a source of pride to you, it shouldn't be a source of shame either.*

It's the love you put into the job that makes it great. Your work should speak for itself. No job can determine your greatness, but your hard work can definitely make your job look great. *Let your work be a source of greatness.* The work should speak for itself. A profession is a profession. Your job is your source of livelihood. Your job is not your identity. You are not alive because you are doing a certain job. Isn't it?

## Change perception to change the things

*We can't do great things but do small things with great love. -Mother Teresa.*

Out of professional compulsions, family pressure, or any other financial constraints, people are forced to continue with their present job. They have to stay with their jobs when they actually want to quit it. Often, you find people complaining that they don't find their job fulfilling, the boss is rude, the salary is not as they expected, or there are not any chances of increment.

The question is that if you don't like your job, and have no other option but to continue the job, then what to do? You are left with only two options, either to change your job or to modify the perception about the job. In other words, if you don't like something, try to change it, or accept it the way it is. The same construction site can be viewed as a mere construction site by one worker. But the same construction site can be viewed as a place of god by another. Likewise, the same patient can be viewed as another patient by the doctor. But the same patient can be viewed as a human being by another medical practitioner. In the end, the way we perceive the things or people makes all the difference.

It is clearly evident that two different persons can have two divergent views. What one finds to be liberating, the other may not find it to be so. What one loves doing, the other might resent doing the same. Ultimately, it's your perception towards the job that matters. Different people would explain the same truth differently. But, the truth remains the same for everybody. It never changes from person to person. Somebody can view the piece of land as an ancestral property while the very same piece of land may be a waste of money by somebody else. In the end, it's our perception towards seeing the things matter.

If you became a farmer because of family compulsions, then change your perception towards it. Instead of grudging about your destiny, try to put your heart into everything you do. Hard work never goes waste. It certainly comes back as an increase in the yield, an increased profit, and a rise in your reputation as a good farmer. To one person, the profession of farming is a job to plow the earth and sow the seeds. To someone else, the very same profession of agriculture is a noble profession that helps feed millions of people in the world.

The profession of teaching can be viewed as a job to teach children by a modest medium called blackboard. The very same job of education can be perceived as a noble profession where you share your valuable knowledge with others. Likewise, the same profession of a doctor can be viewed as a job of prescribing medicines to the patients. The very same profession can be perceived as a noble profession where lives of people are saved. It is very clear that how you view things ultimately becomes your identity. In the end, it your perception towards your profession is the most important thing.

How do we choose between the two different writers who have written articles on the same topic?

What is the difference between a great and an average athlete? Again, what's the difference between a great singer and a mediocre singer? It's the ability to put all your heart into your work that makes you great. If you are a singer, sing so beautifully that your singing becomes your identity. In other words, people should recognize you, by your voice. Your singing should speak for itself.

If you are a chef, prepare food in such a way that your food becomes your identity. In other words, the quality of the food should speak for itself. Likewise, if you are an actor, act so beautifully that people recognize you, by your acting. In other words, your acting should speak for itself. Better do something of value rather than fretting about your destiny. If you have to do something, why not do it whole heartedly rather moaning in grief. In the end, it's all about how you relate yourself to the job.

It's all about loving your profession. Your job should be an extension of yourself.

## How do you judge this?

Whatever you do, your work becomes a projection of yourself. Whether you are working in a restaurant, at office, or in a multi-billionaire company; you create a projection of yourself through your work and vice-versa. Your work becomes your identity. At one point, both are inseparable. You are reflected in your work, and the work gets reflected in you. When both are inseparable, why not pay more attention on how you project yourself to the world.

Take this example. A person is in the job of killing animals for livelihood. The general perception is that the individual is merciless. To the contrary, the person may not be cruel inside; you may find the person to be a kind soul with a caring heart. Labeling someone as brutal because of the chosen profession is certainly wrong. A person is forced to do a particular job because of his inability to find another job. But it is difficult to change the people's way of looking at the things. The point is, at one point of time your profession becomes your identity.

No matter how good you are from within; people identify you by your profession.

Consider this. You work as a waiter. At home, you play many roles. You are a caring husband, a loving father, a responsible son, an elder brother, and a loyal friend. No matter how authoritatively you live at your home, you got to be humble and cooperative at work. People in the hotel should see only the friendly and cooperative side of you. Again, the real person remains hidden to others. Your work has changed your identity. In other words, your profession becomes your identity. You cannot escape it.

Take this example. You might be a top CEO in a multi-millionaire company and earn loads of money. You project yourself as a strict disciplinarian. The only thing that interests you is getting things done at any cost. You might be very humble and friendly person at home, but at office, the image of the strict disciplinarian image becomes your identity. No matter how hard you try to break the existing image, you cannot escape being judged. It's very hard to change the mindset of the people. No matter what the profession, it continues to be your identity. There comes a point when the profession and the professional, merge into one. They become one.

Let your profession become a projection of yourself. Let people identify by your profession, but never let your profession become an identity itself. You are a doctor by profession, but never let the profession become your identity. Likewise, you may work as a painter, a driver, or a cleaner. It is always wise not to identify yourself with your profession. Yes, you may be an artist by profession, but as soon as you step out of your work; you are a human being like everyone else. After you finish your job, return back to your original nature. At home, you play a role of a mother, a father, a wife, a friend and so on and so forth. Never take the tag of the profession so seriously that you forget to be a good human being. In the end, it's the attachment to our identities that brings us the pain. Once we learn to detach ourselves, the pain that comes with the identity also goes away.

*How you judge this?*
*I am not rich.*
*I am not good.*
*I am not at all good.*
*I am a good-for-nothing.*

If you compare yourself with others, it's very likely that you may get hurt in the end. You cannot be best at everything. There is always a possibility that someone else may be more beautiful, rich or more famous than you. In the end, the comparison is likely to give us pain. When it comes to the worldly terms, either you would be ahead or someone else will be ahead of you. There will be someone who has a bigger house than yours or someone who earns more money than you. In other words, some people work for few hours and make lots of money, to the contrary, there are some individuals who work hard but are not able to earn much money. If you go on comparing on the basis of the obvious things, you would be hurting yourself.

Whether we are a farmer, a teacher, or a manager, each one of us is equally needed for the proper functioning of the society. We all work together towards building a better world. We are helping in the nation building. When it comes to the collective contribution towards the nation, everybody is equally contributing their part to create a better world. No contribution is less. Everybody is equally needed for the well-being of a nation.

## Is money more important to you or satisfaction?

A young man wanted to become an artist out of his love for painting. But destiny had other plans. He had a strict and authoritative father. An artist job is not as lucrative as that of an engineer's job. The father intentionally made his son choose an engineering job. As a result, the son became an engineer and started earning loads of money. The deep-seated desire to be an artist got buried. Now, he earns money but not satisfaction. What is more important to you? Whether you love your job for money, or you love the job for satisfaction, the choice is entirely up to you. You have to decide what matters you the most. You have to decide where you see yourself after ten years from now. It's up to you to choose; either to follow your heart to be an artist or to be a company's CEO and be handsomely paid.

It's always in the best interest that you follow your heart.

If you want to achieve money, name, and fame, at the cost of love and peace, you may win in the short run. In the long term, you will have to repent. Money can buy you everything, but not love. You wanted to opt for a career in geology, but you were forced into medical field. Today you are a respectable name in your profession, have a luxurious home, an expensive car and possibly everything one could dream. But, deep inside there is turmoil. The inner turmoil of not being able to do what you wanted to. The pain would last for life-long.

There is no other way to escape it.

## Is this your story?

A woman was a CEO in a multi-million company. She had all the luxuries of life. The latest model of car, an ultra-modern house, a swimming pool, and a gym, she had possibly everything one could think of. She had everything. She had money, fame, home, social status, a successful career, and a loving family. She was successful in every practical term. She often felt proud of her achievements. But, still, something was missing. She lacked her peace of mind. She always felt like being jailed in her own house. She had everything, but couldn't enjoy the riches. There are some things money can't buy. Things like a good laugh, happiness, contentment, peace of mind, and the good old friends are really free in life.

Whether you work in a restaurant, you are a CEO in a multi-millionaire company, or you are a clerk in a small firm, no matter what the job is, the basic aim is to earn livelihood. You want to make enough money so that you can sustain yourself and your family. But the basic quest to do any job remains the same, to earn livelihood.

When you are making your living, why not enjoy the work as well?

You are a doctor, and if you don't like to serve the poor, the weak, and the ill, why become a doctor in the first place? You are a teacher by profession, and you don't like to teach the children, why not be somebody else? You are an engineer, but do not like the ideas of building dams and bridges, why become one in the first place? Why not give the place to someone else who would carry the job wholeheartedly? Better do something you really love rather than resenting from inside. Work should never become a burden in the first place.

Work should be a reflection your joy.

Wouldn't it be meaningful that we choose a profession that projects our true self? If you love children and teaching, why not become a teacher in the first place? Likewise, if you are interested in art and paintings, why not become a painter? Similarly, if you love making food and serving people, why not be a chef? Why not choose a job that makes you happy? Why not choose a right job in the first place itself? We do not listen to the inner voice and follow the crowd.

You are your best judge to decide what the best is for you.

# *HOW PEOPLE JUDGE YOUR CLOTHES*

## Clothes add to the credibility

Dress sense says a lot about a person. How do you think a school going boy should dress? A school going kid should be dressed in his school uniform. Again, how do you think a teenage boy should dress? A teenage boy is supposed to be dressed in vibrant colors of t-shirt and shorts. Likewise, what is the general perception of how an office going person should dress? He should be wearing more decent clothes. In the end, clothes form an extension of our personality.

What is the people's perception towards a doctor? A doctor wears a uniform, an apron and a stethoscope. These things add to the overall image of a physician. In other words, the general people identify a doctor by his uniform. An engineer is identified by his professional uniform. Likewise, an air-hostess can be easily identified by her or his uniform.

Again, how do we identify a policeman, a judge, and a teacher? The answer is, by their respective uniform. What happens when we find a doctor, a lawyer, and a policeman, without their respective uniform? What is our first impression? Would you like to be treated by a doctor who is shoddily dressed, without a proper uniform? It's not the uniform that makes you a doctor, still, the uniform certainly adds to the credibility of the profession. People identify you by the clothes you wear. In other words, your clothes become your identity. Clothes are an extension to your personality.

The way you think, feel, or act would definitely show in the choice of the dressing.

Take this example. You see a man in a well-fitted suit. What is the first thing that comes into your mind by looking at his clothes? We think him to be a decent man. Consider this example. You see a person in the office who is dressed in t-shirt and shorts with dyed hairs. What is the first impression that comes to your mind? We think the person to be an irresponsible person by his way of dressing. The general perception about the clothes of a rock star is that he would be wearing bursting and loud colors. Again, the general perception of a political leader is that he is would be dressed in white attire. Likewise, the general perception of an actress is that she would to be wearing a vibrant colored dress. In other words, we identify a person by the dress he wears.

## Different clothes portray different characters

You must have observed how different people, portray different characters, by wearing different clothes in a film. The character of a wicked mother-in-law is portrayed in a white sari with crooked eyebrows and a spectacle on the nose. The character of the hero is portrayed in colorful trousers and shirts. Again, the character of a heroine is portrayed in beautiful hairstyles and flaunting expensive dresses. Likewise, the character of a villain in the film is portrayed in white shirts and trousers, the black glasses, and a black mole on his right cheek. Isn't it? By looking at the clothes of the characters, the role of a character should come out clearly.

In other words, a villain should look like a villain and a hero should look like a hero. The characters express different emotions and moods. After all, you cannot make all the characters, wear the same dress throughout the whole film.

It's clearly evident that in order to display different emotions, we have to dress differently. When we are sad, we dress up with dull colors. When we are happy, we dress up with bright colors. It's evident that emotions play a significant role in determining how we dress. If a person likes to wear branded clothes, the expensive accessories, the beauty parlor, or a salon, is a matter of one's personal choice. There is absolutely no harm in dressing well. The problem arises when we mistake clothes with our real identity. The expensive clothes, the makeup, and the hairstyle, all constitute the part of our outer self. These outwardly things must not be confused with inner self or inner peace. The clothes are an extension to our personality, but not the personality in itself. Clothes do not define a person rather than the person wearing them defines them. The clothes constitute a part of your outwardly reality. Clothes shouldn't be confused with your identity.

A rogue may dress convincingly in a well-fitted suit. But, we mistake the person as a gentleman because of external appearance. In fact, a decently dressed person may or may not be a gentleman. It is precisely where the people are mistaken, taking the external and the obvious things to be true. It can lead to disastrous results. It is not that wearing nice and expensive clothes is wrong, but to conclude the whole picture by the clothes alone is certainly not noble. Things that appear on the surface are not always as they appear to be. There is always a greater truth lying beneath to it.

## How you judge this?

A general perception that a woman who works in a bar is not a moral person is certainly wrong. Like any other human being, the woman working in a bar is a human being first. Like any other profession, it is a profession first. Does a person's way of dressing alone make a person immoral? There may be many reasons why a person chooses to wear a certain dress. Professional compulsions or due to her personal choice, a woman might be wearing a particular dress. In the end, clothes do not define morality. Acts define morality. A woman who works in a bar has to be immoral is a highly appalling view. The real person behind the clothes might actually be a different person than we assume her to be. The way a person chooses to dress is one's personal matter.

In the end, it's our quality of thoughts that define our acts and finally define whether we are moral or not. An immoral person from within may cleverly conceal his or her wickedness by dressing modestly. Anyone could mistake such a person for a modest being. But, the greater truth is that you cannot hide the real person inside for long. In the end, the true person inside will find a way to reveal itself. In the end, our own thoughts define our acts. Our own acts define morality. Defining morality on the basis of a person's profession is certainly a gross injustice. An incorrect consideration always gives an incorrect conclusion. Clothes do not define a person rather than a person wearing them defines them. In the end, it is one's way of thinking rather than one's way of dressing that define morality.

## The clothes say it all

The way a person dresses has a deep connection with his inner feelings, emotions, and attitudes. Different emotions lead to a different way of dressing. The way we dress has an impact on our inner feelings. Likewise, our inner feelings have profound implications on the way we dress. How does a movie portray the character of a gangster? A gangster is seen dressed in shirts and trousers of typical colors, wearing black spectacles with heavy moustache and a gun in hand.

Again, if you see a person who has intentionally dressed like a gangster, what would you think? You may think that either he is a gangster or wants to portray like one. The psychology behind a person intentionally trying to portray a don's image is to succeed in frightening people. The idea is to scare people so that the person can run his business smoothly. The basic truth is that the business of a gangster strives on his ability to scare people. If the thug wants to succeed in frightening people, the gangster has to dress accordingly. In other words, our clothes are a medium to project ourselves. We are identified by the clothes we wear. It's an established fact that our deepest emotions are reflected in the way we dress. We see a person well-dressed in a suit, driving a luxurious car, and enjoying a multi-millionaire status, we quickly assume that the person might be a good human being. What you see outside may be to the total contrast to what's inside. Assumptions are assumptions. It may or may not be the truth. In the end, a person's emotions play a major role regardless of the way of dressing. Clothes convey the subliminal message that we want to deliver.

*It is very clear that our feelings are reflected in the way we wear our clothes, and inversely our clothes are a reflection of our inner feelings. In other words, clothes define the emotions.*

A person's emotions play a major role in deciding what message one wants to convey by wearing a particular dress.

## How would you judge this?

Yes, dressing appropriately will improve your social presence. People will view you as someone who is serious towards his profession. Dressing properly will build an air of credibility and trust around you. A person dressed properly would instill confidence in the people. For the same reason, every profession has a dress code. It helps building an air of credibility and trust among the people. Hence, there is a dress code for doctors, lawyer, and teacher and the other professions.

A person who comes for an interview shoddily dressed is likely to be rejected. Among the other things that are being considered for an interview, the clothes of the participant are an important factor too. Consider this example. There are two different candidates appearing for an interview. One is nicely dressed with newly bought clothes and the second one is dressed shoddily without even having the dress ironed. What is the first impression? We get an impression that the second candidate has not taken the interview seriously. Otherwise, why would he appear so poorly for the interview? Again, it is a whole different issue whether the first candidate is as promising as he appears to be. Likewise, the second candidate might actually be very knowledgeable, kind, and understanding. But due to his poor dressing sense, the final verdict goes against him.

We are identified by our clothes, but clothes shouldn't become an identity in itself. A good person might dress up shoddily, and a bad person might dress up nicely. If you are judging someone entirely upon the external appearances, you are definitely missing the larger picture. The greater truth remains hidden.

## How you judge a woman who has a poor self-image?

Take this example. There is a woman who has a poor image of herself. She thinks that nobody would be interested in dating her. Out of desperation, she intentionally wears a dress that would draw attention of the people. In other words, the woman wants love and *not necessarily* wants sex. Yes, the surface truth is that the woman is wearing clothes to draw attention. The deeper truth is that the woman desperately needs love and care. It is the deeper truth which the most people cannot see.

Morality has got nothing to do with the how a person dresses. It has got more to do with what the person actually holds in his heart. There are many people who wear nice and decent clothes, but they are not at all moral. The problem definitely doesn't lay with the way a person chooses to dress in a certain way. The problem lies in the way; we interpret the person's choice of wearing a dress.

There is no denying the fact that your clothes are your identity, but they shouldn't be mistaken for the identity itself. The point is, there is more to a person that the clothes he is wearing. Clothes do not define a person rather than the person defines them. Giving too much importance to the way of dressing will lead to the overshadowing of the real person inside. Clothes do not define morality. Our acts do. We are always mistaken by the things that appear on the surface. We see something on the surface and immediately jump to conclusions. The problem lies in the wrong interpretation.

# *HOW PEOPLE JUDGE YOUR MARRIAGE*

## How would you judge this?

*The single status of a person vs. married status.*

Marriage is considered to be a union of two hearts, two souls, and two families. How does marriage affect the married couples? As far as the woman's point of view is concerned, everything changes. The home, the family, the relationship, the way of thinking, and even her surname changes for the woman. Of course, here I am not talking about the women who like to keep their maiden names post marriage.

When a person is single, one can live the way one loves to, eat anything one likes to, can do anything one pleases to, and wear whatever one likes to wear. But, things change drastically after the marriage. With Marriage comes the responsibility. The time to wake up, the eating habit, the way of spending money, the relationships, and the responsibilities, everything changes drastically. You no longer remain the person, you were before the marriage. Similar changes are can be seen in your partner as well. Your partner also tries to change his ways of living.

In the end, a marriage is a single mold for two different people, with different mind-sets, and two distinct cultures.

You are trying to fit into one single mold called the marriage. A vegetarian gets married to a non-vegetarian. What is the result? It changes the eating habits. Similarly, a spendthrift is married to a miser. It changes the spending habits. Again, if an outgoing personality is married to an introvert. It leads to the change in the social habits. In other words, marriage is like a chemical reaction to produce an entirely different product in the end.

When two completely different people come together, it is very likely that they both would influence each other. A definite change can be seen in both the partners. To make the marriages work, the non-vegetarian switches to a vegetarian diet. An alcohol-addict begins abstaining from alcohol; a lazy person begins working harder, an atheist turns into a religious person, and an outgoing person becomes an introvert. Sacrifices from both the sides are necessary to make things work. After all, you cannot expect a bicycle to run smoothly on a single tire? Isn't it? When two people come together and work so hard to make their marriages work, it really hurts when things don't go as planned.

## You cannot escape being judged?

If you are single, you would be accessed for the reasons for being single. Again, if you choose to have a married life, you would be judged for the reasons for being married. If you decide to be married and have kids, you would be judged for it. Likewise, if you chose to be married and not have kids, you would be judged. The whole point is that you cannot escape being judged. There is no other way. You cannot escape being judged by people. Every aspect of your life gets subjected to people's scrutiny.

Whether it's the question to get married or not, or it is the question to have kids or not; it is up to the person to decide the best. You are best judge to decide what is good for you and what is not. It is a highly personal question whether an individual should consider staying in or opting out of a marriage. No matter what you choose to do, you would be judged. No one has ever escaped being judged. Then, why bother about what people would say?

## How do you judge this?

*How's the marriage going on?*
*Why are you not thinking of having kids?*
*You should consult a good gynecologist.*
*Perhaps you should visit our spiritual master.*

## Whether or not others are in the same boat as you?

Take this example. There are some people who are overly curious to know what is going in other person's married life. A woman would ask one particular question to everyone she met. How was their children's married life going on? While some would say that the children's marriage was doing well, some would say that their children's marriage was not doing well. What the woman was actually trying to ascertain, whether she was alone in her despair or were there some other people. She would mentally access whether others were sailing in the same boat or not. If I am happily single, I won't be interested in finding the status of the other person. Likewise, if I am happy with my married life, I won't be too curious to know about other person's marital life.

Later, it comes out that her own daughter was leading an unhappy married life, and she was trying to seek some comfort through the other peoples' problems.

The thing is if I am really happy with my married life, I won't be too curious to know the details of others married life. It's only when people who themselves are unhappy, they try to find out people having similar problems. In other words, it is like one single person, seeking another single individual for emotional support. Again, it is like one married person, seeking another married person for emotional support.

## When things don't go as planned

When there is mounting pressure from the families to make the marriages work, getting divorce is seen as something against the society. No matter how much effort people put in to save their marriages, the end results surely hurts. There might be many reasons for continuing the marriage –social stigma, the family pressure, and the responsibilities of children and so on. Despite the decaying relation, often, people pretend to the world that they are happily married.

Someday, one finds that there is something that is missing in the marriage. When the marriage does not work as planned, people turn to the person outside the wedding. In the hope of getting acceptance, people turn to the other people. They try to seek the happiness; they think they have been deprived of, as an individual. It is precisely when infidelity, adultery, affairs, and out-of-marriage sex happen. The earlier blissful state of married life now turns into blame-game.

When you think of opting out or staying in the marriage, think of the reasons for getting married in the first place. In other words, you wanted happiness, so you got married. Everybody gets married for the want of love, but soon find themselves surrounded with full of the other troubles. Instead of blaming others for your despair, have a deep introspection first. Try to find out your weaknesses. Work on your weaknesses, so that it turns into your strengths. Only a thorough introspection would lead to a blissful marriage. In the end, it's the peace of mind that matters the most. In the end, everyone seeks happiness.

# *HOW WE JUDGE OURSELVES*

## We judge ourselves through the eyes of others

Often, we see ourselves through the eyes of others. In fact, we perceive ourselves by the way, the other people see us. Rarely do we come across a person, who has his own vision and judgment of seeing things. It is very clear that our way of seeing the things would ultimately decide our way of judging them. We see people, things, and the circumstances, and we judge them according to our way of seeing things. We keep on scrutinizing the things. Basically, we decide to see, who is more immaculately dressed, who is richer, or who is happier. When we find ourselves to be better than others, we are happy. This constant scrutiny over others gives us a sense of fulfillment, pleasure, and achievement. In any case, we always want ourselves to be better.

In fact, the very basic purpose of judging is to find faults in other. We want to feel better. So, we judge. In fact, to judge is like finding a shorter pencil, so that our pencil turns out to be taller. Judging someone is the same. If we are always judging others, there are just two possibilities, either something wrong lies in us or something is wrong in our approach.

Between too much of love and hate, lies a thin line. Between too much of confidence and under-confidence, again, lies a thin line. Similarly, whether it is excess of love, overeating, or extreme happiness, it leads to the path of destruction. In the end, any attempt to cross the line is going to hurt our self. Anything in excess is never good. With too much confidence, we begin to overlook everything. Too little confidence leads us to constantly doubt everything. In the end, too much of anything would ultimately hurt us the most. We never strive to try to reach a point of balance. In the end, it is the equanimity that helps us sail through.

## How do you judge this?

*I am too good.*
*Nobody can beat me.*
*No one is as good as me.*
*I can achieve anything I want.*
*I am good at everything*
*I am simply the best.*
*No one rejects me.*

## Do you judge yourself as not good enough?

If you judge yourself as not good enough, believe me, you are not the only one.

I am also just like you. Like everyone else, I often doubt myself. Whenever there is some challenging task, I begin to doubt myself that if I would be able to do it. Even after successfully overcoming many hurdles, I still doubt my abilities. Later, I realized that unless a deep introspection is done, the negative pattern continues to block the buoyancy of a person. In other words, I had blocked my own progress. Judging yourselves harshly and excessive doubting is detrimental for the well-being of a person. While it's good to doubt, it's certainly not good to always keep doubting. Unless you learn to believe in yourself, you cannot believe in anything else.

## How do you judge this?

*Would I be able to do it?*
*Are others way ahead of me?*
*What if I fail?*
*What will people think of me?*
*Would I never be as good as others?*
*Am I good at nothing?*
*I won't be able to achieve anything.*
*I am a loser.*
*I look awkward.*
*Nobody loves me.*

## Do you judge that god wants you to suffer?

Some people who think that God wants them to suffer. God forbid, if we are born with a physical deformity or mental retardation, how do we think of ourselves? We would be spending our whole life in blaming ourselves. Either we would be blaming ourselves or blaming god for our condition. People go on punishing themselves, thinking that God wants them to be punished.

Some people would even go further by blaming their previous lives, for their suffering they are enduring today. People can get immensely cruel when it comes to those are not like them. When it comes to people with any type of disability, the general perception towards them is not good. Whether said consciously or unconsciously; an insensitive remark can tremendously hurt someone who is already trying to fight against all odds.

People do not readily accept someone who is not like them. An insensitive remark from anyone could cause grave mental agony. When someone is already in need of help, we leave them. It hurts to find that you are not normal like everybody else. It hurts to find that you would never be able to achieve, what everybody else can. The worst part is to think that God wants you to suffer. This leads to the worst kind of guilt pattern that one finds hard to break. Whether it's defect by birth, a life endangering illness, or some other serious issue, an insensitive remark can certainly aggravate the pain to another level.

Take this example. A child is born with mental retardation. The mother loves the child with all her might, no matter what people would have to say. But, when the mother thinks of the insensitive remarks that come from the people, it brings her down to tears. Instead of helping someone who is in need, people carelessly comment and leave. The real problem is that people do not readily accept someone who is not like them. People have a tendency of making fun of those who they don't consider normal like them. The pain gets increased manifold by people's insensitive remarks. By carelessly making remarks, we might be depriving someone of his hope. Sometimes, it is the hope which provides courage to fight and survive.

Sometimes, we hurt ourselves hurt like no other person can. It is the attachment towards the suffering that causes hurt in the end; and not the suffering itself. If you are able to detach yourself from the suffering, you can be free of it. The more attached you are to the suffering; the more likely you are to suffer. In the end, it is the attachment that brings suffering. The Buddhism teaches a beautiful concept of *detachment*. Detachment is the practice of not getting attached, to anyone or anything, in general. Detachment does not mean that you have to see someone in pain, and still do not do anything about it. Detachment means that you practice seeing the pain without getting attached to the pain itself. The pain would still be there, but the attachment towards the pain will start diminishing. In the end, it's our own attachment towards the pain, and not the pain itself, that leads to the further pain. The more attached you will be, the more you have to suffer. The less attached you will be, the less you have to suffer.

Every great soul has taught us the values of compassion, love, peace, and forgiveness. When it comes to applying these virtues, we never ensue. Love is abundantly available, but we fail to identify it. When we feel dearth of love, we turn to other people for seeking love. When people turn their back, we get hurt. Love yourselves first. You cannot confer love unless you have it yourself. Love that comes from within is the love that shines on the outside. Unless you believe in yourselves first, no one else will believe in you. Likewise, unless you love yourselves first, no one else will love you.

## How would you judge this?

*I am a poor soul.*
*Oh god is so cruel.*
*God has punished me so much.*
*Life is so difficult for me.*
*What a pity?*
*I am a child of a lesser god.*
*God wants me to suffer.*
*God has punished me.*
*God has put me into never ending hell.*

## Is it not true?

*Is it not true that when we are too happy with ourselves, we are just busy enjoying our lives? It is only when we get hurt; we step out to help others.*

Remember the time when you had everything – love, money, home, luxuries, and good health. Did you take the pain to reach out those who were not as lucky as you were? Did you feed the hungry? Did you quench a thirsty person? The answer is a big NO. It's only when we are in some kind of pain or trouble; we begin to feel compassion towards others. It's only when we feel the wound ourselves; we step out to help the others.

Unless you step into others' shoes, you can never fully understand what it's like to the other person. One can never really understand the feelings of a sufferer, unless one goes through the same pain oneself. It's only when we ourselves get a hurtful setback; we begin to feel for those who going through the same pain. If the hurt is able to evoke compassion in you, then the same hurt should be considered a blessing.

Suffering can be a means to make us better human beings.

# *WHAT IS YOUR WAY OF DEFINING THESE?*

## According to you, what is the best way to take decisions?

We are always leaning on other people to help us in making decisions. Sometimes, we blindly lean onto others for our decisions. When it comes to finding a suitable job, we turn to others. Again, when it comes to finding a suitable life partner, we turn to others for help. Whether it is finding a suitable home, finding a good school for our children, or deciding whether you want to go ahead with a life-risking surgery or not, we depend heavily on others for our decisions.

There is no denying the fact that it is good to take advice from others as they may be well experienced than us. The point is a valid one. There is nothing wrong in turning to others for help, but it is certainly wrong to depend heavily on someone else for all your decisions. In the end, others may decide things for you, but you alone have to decide what lies in your greater interest.

Even if you are leaning on other people for your decisions, no matter how experienced a person is, the decisions can still be wrong. No one can predict with exact certainty whether a particular decision is going to be right or not. No matter how many successful surgeries you have performed in the past, with every new upcoming surgery there comes the possibility of the newer risks. Similarly, no matter how successfully you have climbed a mountain, every time you begin afresh, arise its own challenges and surprises. Life is all about taking the new challenges every time again and again. Everyone makes mistakes. After all, it's human to make mistakes.

The thing that frightens us the most is the degree of uncertainty with every subsequent decision. Every decision is associated with the risks; it brings along with it when you take the decisions. Before taking the decisions, you have to take into the consideration the risks involved in it. We want to take the decisions, but do not want to accept the risks that it brings along with it. In the end, no decision comes without risks. As a movie director, you have to decide whether you want to cast an entirely new comer for your film or to go with an already established actor. While an already established star seems to be a better choice as the success is almost guaranteed, but the end results may be promising if a newcomer is given a chance. In the end, the risk is involved in both the cases. It is the uncertainty of the results that make us frightful. It is always in the individual's best interest that he decides for himself, what is good for him and what is not.

Similarly, it is up to the publisher to decide, if he wants to choose an already established author for his next project or a first time writer. Again, when we choose an already established author, the choice seems to be safe. With the little-known writer, the choice may be a risky bet. In the end, it is for the publisher to decide whether he wants to go with the guarantee path to success or the risky one. It is in the best interest for the person to determine what lies in his greater interest.

Likewise, the decision whether to marry a girl by your parent's choice or to marry someone of our own choice is entirely up to you. The parent's choice may seem to be right, as the decision comes from people who have an enormous amount of experience with them. Again, if you want to marry the girl of your choice, it is entirely up to you. You have to accept the uncertainty that comes along with the decision. It is always in the best that a person takes his own decisions by carefully considering all the risks involved. No one can guarantee you with the end results. Either thing would go as expected or they would not. People can help you in making decision, but no one can accurately construe a decision that can offer guaranteed success in the end.

My primary aim behind writing this book is to make more and more people aware of themselves. In the end, it is your life. We cannot succeed in the examination of life by copying someone else's answers. No matter how risky it is, in the end, you alone have to take your decisions. Fearing the end results, we shy of making decisions. Either way, you are at risk. If we decide to go the guaranteed way, there may be risk involved in it. The book written by an established author may or may not be a hit. Similarly, if we want to go the risky way, the final outcome may be uncertain, too. Contrarily, a book written by a relatively unknown author may become a massive hit. In the end, it is your life, so it should be you to decide what lies in your greater interest.

No matter how many times you get it wrong, you have to keep taking your own decisions. When you completely accept the responsibilities that come along with the decisions, you begin to take the charge of your life as well. The best thing about taking your own decisions is that you will not have anyone else to blame for your miseries. Again, the best thing about taking your own decisions is that you won't be having anybody else to blame, if at all something goes wrong. If everything goes as planned, you would be happy for your all life, and if things don't go as planned you will acquire an experience. Instead of finding someone else to blame for your miseries, you should take the responsibilities on your shoulders and move ahead in life. Instead of blaming someone else for your miseries, it is better to accept your responsibilities and to learn from the mistakes and be wiser.

In other words, no matter how many times you have succeeded in making correct decisions, you have to start all over again while taking a fresh decision. You cannot always be sure that your choices and decisions would be right. In fact, there is no formula to ensure that your decisions would prove right. No one can you guarantee that things will work. What works for someone else might not work for you. In fact, you cannot question why something is working for someone and not for you.

If someone succeeds in losing 30 lbs of weight in few months, it doesn't mean that you would be able to do the same, too. Every person is different with a different body type. What works for one may not work for another.

People can decide things for you, but it's you to accept the responsibilities in the end. If the decision is right, then it is your responsibility. Again, if the decision is wrong, then it is your responsibility too. We ask people whether we are beautiful or not? We turn to people to decide whether we are looking good in a particular dress or not. Again, when it comes to taking more serious decisions, we lean onto others. People can help you with the decisions, but you alone have to decide what is right for you. It is the uncertainty that comes with the decision that makes it a frightening experience. We turn to other people for choosing us a life partner. But, there is no guarantee that the decision may turn right. In the end, either you might end up with a happy married life or a miserable life. No one can precisely predict the accuracy of the decisions.

## How would you judge this?

*In the name of helping us, sometimes, the people around us are too willing to assist us with their advices.*

While it is good that people are ready to help us, but it is certainly not good that one is too dependent upon others. Too much leaning towards others for help would hamper your own growth. It creates an impression that you are not capable of doing anything on your own. In the end, it creates a poor image of self. You begin to lack confidence. In the end, depending too much upon others for your own well-being would hurt you. You are left with more doubts for yourself.

Take this example. You want to learn swimming. How would you learn it? You try to learn all techniques of swimming by diligently following the instructor. Though someone else can help you with the all the techniques, still, it is left to you to decide whether you are willingly accepting the instructions or not. No matter how difficult it seems for you, no one else can make you swim if you are not willing to learn it yourself.

In other words, people can show you the path, but cannot make you walk on the path. You have to walk on your own. Similarly, no matter how good the instructor is, unless you try to practice yourself, even the best teacher is of little good. No matter how valuable advice someone gives to you, it is useless, unless you put it into the practice. In the end, it's the individual person's own efforts and willingness to learn something that makes him proficient in any field.

Decision making is similar to learning swimming or any other activity. In the end, you have to decide how diligently you want to learn the techniques of swimming and finally take your own decisions. The same teacher teaches to the whole class, but not every student passes. While some student would pass with good grades, some would fare with the average grades, and some would even fail. In the end, it is the students own willingness to learn what has been taught matters.

Unless a student is willing to learn, a teacher cannot make someone learn. You are your best judge to decide how you are going to take your decisions. No other person can do it for you. Of course, there is nothing wrong in asking for help, still, it's you to decide what is good for you and what is not.

## How is your definition of success?

What is the definition of success? Different people have different answers. For some people, success means inner peace and tranquility. For others, it is equivalent to material gain and prosperity. In other words, how you perceive things is clearly reflected in the way you would define them. Likewise, it is clearly evident that the way you define things would be reflected in the way you perceive them.

Success means material gains to some people. Such people are always busy finding to achieve material gains and money. For them, success is equivalent to be able to earn more money. Contrarily, to some people, material gain means nothing. These people are in the search of life's greater truths. The gain in the worldly terms is immaterial to them. No two individuals have the same definition for the same term. Different people define the same truth differently. It all depends on your way of perceiving things. The way you perceive things clearly reflects in the way you judge the things.

Success means different to different people.

People define the same success differently. In search of the greater pursuits like inner peace and tranquility, some people have left everything. By literally abandoning huge amounts of money, some people are in the search of their peace of mind. An enlightened person would judge a man with materialistic desires as foolish. Contrarily, a man seeking worldly desires will judge an enlightened soul as foolish. You just cannot lay a uniform set of rules and regulations for everyone. Success for some means gaining material gains while success means achieving inner peace for other. In other words, there is no hard and fast rule for defining success. Whether success means materialistic pleasures or it means the inner peace, you are your best judge to decide. There is no correct way to define success. It's up to you to decide what success means to you. No other person can decide it for you. It's up to you to decide whether you want to earn material gains or inner peace. You are your best judge to decide what is good for you.

## What is your definition of money? Is money important or the way it is earned is important?

Let's consider this example. A person wants to earn a lot of money. He works day in and day out. He dreams having his own house, a vehicle, and other financial securities. Now he works hard to sustain his family and dreams of having some money. He wants to earn money by the legitimate means. Now my question to you is, is there something wrong in dreaming of money and acquiring it by the legitimate means? You would say that what's wrong with it.

Another person wants to earn money, no matter what the source of money. In other words, he wants to earn money at any cost. Be it gambling; drug trafficking, smuggling, or even killing. This way of earning money is definitely wrong, but there are people who continue to earn the money in this way. Money is all that matters, for some people. The illegitimate activities may include drug trafficking, or corruption, or the unlawful activities. The source of money doesn't matter to some people until they are gaining benefits from it.

It is clearly evident that earning money through legitimate means is important for some while money is important for other. Whether success means earning money through the legitimate means or the illegitimate means, is all up to you. No other person can decide it for you. There is no single rule for everybody but one rule equally applies to everybody alike. You are free to choose the means of earning money, but you are not free to escape the consequences that it brings along with it. You have to bear the consequences. In other words, the law of free-will says that you are free to choose, but you are not free to escape its consequences.

## What is your definition of marriage?

If you ask people the reason for getting married, they all would reply differently. In other words, different people would define marriage differently. Some would answer, for sex. Some would reply for the want of love and affection. Again, some would like to get married because they don't want to live a lonely life. Likewise, some would like to get married in a hope of getting dowry. Again, some would want to get married because they want to equal the score against someone.

Likewise, some people would want to get married because their parents want them to get settled. Then, there are some who want to get married because their elders approved someone for them. Again, some people would want to get married because someone closed to them wanted to see them married. Some would want to get married for the want of kids. Again, some would like to get married because the society wants them to. Likewise, some would want to get married because they want to grow old together.

It is very clear that different people have different reasons for getting married. No two individuals get married for the same reason.

When asked to define a successful marriage, getting married to someone of their choice means success to some people. Likewise, staying in the marriage means success to some people. It's very clear that different people have different reasons for getting married.

In other words, you would be getting what you were searching for in your mind. If you are in pursuit of sex alone, you would get a life-partner exactly like that. If you are in search of love, you would be getting a loving partner. And if you want to get married for dowry, you would be getting money but not love.

In other words, your life partner would be the exact reflection of your wishes and desires. In other words, you would get what you want. No other person is responsible for your choice of partner, but you alone. It's solely up to you to decide why you want to get married in life. You have to decide what qualities you seek in your life partner. No other person is responsible for your choice. You are your best judge to decide. If you think that marriage is a divine medium for seeking peace, it's entirely your choice. Again, if marriage is a means of fulfilling the material gains in the life, it's your choice. You are your best judge to decide whether you want to stay single or want to get married. Again, you are your best judge to decide whether you want to stay in the marriage or opt out of the marriage. No other person can decide it for you.

## What is your definition of land?

It is very clear that different people may view the same land differently. How you see things is going to reflect in the way you judge things. If you view the land as a property investment option, it's your judgment. Again, if you view the land as your ancestral property, it's entirely your judgment. Nothing can be done against it. No other person can choose something on your behalf. You have to make choices of your life. You are your best judge to decide as how you are going to judge the piece of land. Nobody else can decide it for you what is the right definition.

Different people would define the same piece of land differently. For a farmer, the land is his source of earning income. The same land may be merely a property investment to other. Again, the same land may be an ancestral property with sentimental value to other. To an industrialist, the same land might be an opportunity to build buildings.

Different people would view the same thing differently.

## What is your definition of healthy body?

Think about the definition of healthy body. Different people would define the concept of healthy body differently. To some individuals, a healthy body means a plump body. Others would define a fit and muscular body to be a healthy body. Again, some people would define that a healthy body is about having a lot of energy and stamina. A doctor would determine a body to be healthy when it matches all the health parameters. A labor defies a healthy body as being fit enough to carry enough load on his back. Again, a wrestler defines a healthy body as being fit enough to win over his opponent in the - the bout. For an athlete, a healthy body means being able to run like nobody else can. For a weight lifter, a healthy body means to be able to carry a lot of weights. For a swimmer, a healthy body means to able to swim like nobody else can.

In other words, different people would define the same truth, differently. In fact, you cannot say that which definition for the healthy body is complete in every aspect. Every person defines the same truth differently. If you perceive a hard-working body as a healthy body, then it's solely your judgment. You are your best judge to decide. You have to decide. If you think that skinny means healthy, then it's your judgment. If you think that plump means healthy, then it's your judgment. No other person can decide what is good for you. You are your best judge.

## What is your definition of beauty?

The dictionary meaning of beautiful is attractive, cute, nice-looking, pleasant, alluring and so on. Do you allow people to judge whether you are beautiful or not? Are you dependent on others to make you feel beautiful? Each one of us would describe the word beautiful differently. It also means that different people see the same thing differently. The point is, what one may find to be beautiful, the other may not. When we ask someone about how we look, there are possibilities of only two things. Either you are fully aware that you are beautiful and seek a complement or you are in doubt about yourself and seek encouraging words.

Some people consider that being fair is beautiful while some consider dusky as beautiful. Each one has one's own definition. Some people consider a plump body to be beautiful while others don't. Some people like to wear a lot of ornaments while others don't. It's strange that we ask to others whether we are beautiful or not. Nobody else can help you if you don't love yourself. Unless you come out of your old negativity pattern, nothing would help. It's not about seeking others' opinion on being beautiful alone. It applies to a lot of other issues as well.

It is clearly evident that the definition of beauty changes from people to people. Each one has one's own definition. Is the mother who toils hard not beautiful? Is the old grandmother not beautiful who made sacrifices for the entire family? Is the neighborhood aunt not beautiful who makes goodies for everyone without expecting anything in return? By which definition of beautiful would you go? Would it not be better that we stick to our own definitions of beauty. Until you think yourself to be beautiful; nobody else can make you feel beautiful. The thing is, you are your best judge to decide whether you are beautiful or not. If you think you are beautiful, you are beautiful. The whole thing comes down to just one thing; nobody else can make you feel their way.

## What is your definition of the best food eating habit?

Consider the food eating habits of the people. While some people consider vegetarian food to be the best, some people consider non-vegetarian food to be the best. The people advocating the vegetarian food say that practicing vegetarianism helps follow the principles of non-violence. Practicing vegetarianism has many beneficial effects, the fat content of the body gets drastically reduced, and it also brings us peace of mind as no animal was killed for the food. In other words, people practicing vegetarianism advocate the beneficial effects it brings along with it. Going vegetarianism helps the planet become greener, it helps the reduction in the carbon dioxide content in the atmosphere, and a lot of trees are being saved from getting cut.

Contrarily, those practicing non-vegetarianism advocate that it's for the religious reasons that they practice non-vegetarianism. Some advocate that non-vegetarian food is simply tastier than the vegetarian food. Others advocate that non-vegetarian food is a good source of protein for them. Practicing non-vegetarianisms is a great source of body building for some. While some people eat non-vegetarian food just because they feel everyone else is eating the same. No two people define the same truth in a similar way.

If you think that going vegetarian is good for you, it's your judgment. On the contrary, if you think that going non-vegetarian is good for you, it's your judgment. You are your best judge to decide what is good for you. No other person can judge it for you. You have to come with a choice.

## How would you judge this?

Take an example of body organ donation. There are a lot of controversies surrounding it. The people against the concept advocate that if you donate your eyes in this life time, you would come up as a blind person in the next birth. Though there are no scientific evidences to such claims, still, some people believe in such concepts. Again, there are people who say that the very concept itself is against their religious sentiments. Though their concept against organ donation is wrong, it is difficult to make people change their mindset. It would take a long time to change the mindset of the people.

Contrarily, people advocating the concept say that it has got nothing to do with hurting the religious sentiments, but it has more to do with saving someone's precious life. It is a noble concept and a way towards immorality. The person who chooses to donate continues to live even after one's death. However, it needs to gain a wider acceptance, and it will take a long time to make general people aware of the concept.

## What is your definition of morality?

What is morality according to you? Different people would define it differently. The dictionary defines the term morality as the principles concerning the distinction between the right and wrong, and good or bad behavior. In other words, morality is ethics. There cannot be a rigid definition of morality. It is hard to define morality in one single definition; we may sometimes come across many contradictions.

For instance, take the case of the dress code for woman. People wear clothes according to their culture and religion. Some cultures are more liberal and allow woman to wear clothes without many restrictions, and some cultures that instruct their woman to wear clothes with modesty. The dress a woman chooses to wear is a matter of her own faith and her rights.

A woman in a fashionable clothes and makeup can be as moral and respectable as any other woman. Morality comes from within. It has nothing to do with outward things. Labeling a woman as moral or immoral because of the choice of her clothes is certainly wrong. A person's way of looking at the things would decide how a person's belief would be molded. If women are being treated with great respect in a family, naturally the children would also respect women in their later lives. If women are disrespected, emotionally abused, or physically tortured, it is more likely that the precedent has been already set for the children. In the end, it is your own way of thinking that makes you great. Your clothes do not define morality, but your acts define morality.

The general misconception that a woman herself has asked for trouble by wearing a fashionable clothes or wear makeup is certainly wrong. Why do the countries, where women are seen dressed with modesty encounter sexual crimes? Clothes do not define morality, but the quality of a person's thoughts certainly does. In the end, any person is free to wear the clothes one wishes to wear. Morality has nothing to do with the way a person choose to wear, eat, or act. Morality is more defined by a person's quality of thoughts rather than one's outwardly appearances of a person.

## What is your definition of religion?

Does any religion ask its people to kill in the name of god? Is it not an immoral thing to kill someone, and claim that you were doing it in the name of god at the later stage? No religion has ever asked its followers to kill innocent people. Still, people kill one another. Later, people claim that they did it in the name of religion and to please God.

Every religion asks its people not to steal, not to judge, not to kill, not to lie or give false testimony, and not to commit adultery. Likewise, every religion asks its people to love one's neighbor as oneself and be reconciled. No religion asks its followers to commit adultery, but people still commit it. Again, No religion asks people to give false testimony, but still people lie. Likewise, no religion asks to kill one another or steal, but contrary to these teachings, people kill others and steal.

It is the people who modify the teachings of the religion for their own convenience, and then justify themselves later. People claim that they were carrying it in the name of god. People do not accept the truth the way it is, and modify the truth according to their needs at the later stage. When modified, truth doesn't remain truth. It becomes modified truth. Unless we consider the truth without doing any additions or subtractions to it, we cannot know the whole truth. Every religion preaches its people to do the right things; still, people modify these teachings and do the wrong for their own convenience.

In general terms, each person defines truth according to his or her needs and modifies them for the sake of conveniences. What one person finds to be true the other person may not? Again, it is imperative that one must keep checking whether one is on the right track or not. Whether one wants to accept the truth in its purest form or whether one wants to modify the truth, is all up to the individual. It should be noted that the individual is not free to escape the consequences that comes along with the modified truth. It's best left to a person to decide how they want to live their lives.

## What is your definition of honesty?

How to judge whether what is true and what is false? Is it so difficult to speak the truth in the today's world? A trader is not telling the complete truth about his products. A particular advertising company is not telling its clients the entire truth about the products.

Practically speaking, it is a tough job to speak the truth, but certainly is not impossible. One may find that people who go the deceitful way of earning money make more profit. A dishonest merchant selling substandard products to its customers is able to make a lot of profit. It is very easy to get influenced and to follow his ways of making the money.

Take this example. A person employed in a government sector finds out that he can easily make money by corruption and still not get caught. The temptation to earn money becomes primary. The person makes money by all means; later on justifying in the name of his wife and children. He thinks that because of the money he earned, his family is happy. Years go by, and stacks of money fill his house. Then comes a time when there is no place to keep the money. And as they say all good things come to an end. An enquiry reveals his wrong doings. Everything is lost the money, the self-respect, and the dignity. Were these temporary comforts worth the pain that it brought along with it in the long run? Is choosing the wrong way justified in the end?

Yes, dishonesty or lying may bring you profit in the short run. One may find it tempting to go the dishonest way. As it begins to bring profit, people even begin to justify these methods. It may be tempting to do what we feel everybody else is doing. When we see how easily people deceive and escape, going the deceitful way seems to be even more tempting. In the long term, you have to pay the price. In the end, you lose everything; your peace of mind, the respect, and the credibility. Once you lose your credibility, it cannot come back. Forever these things are lost. You are the best judge to decide whether you want to gain money through honest means or lose your precious peace of mind by going the dishonest way.

## Think about it for a moment

Life is a series of puzzle, one after the other. There are many twists and turns. Many times there comes the situation when you have no other choice but to decide. You have to come up with a judgment, whether you like it or not. Life judges us. Everyone according to their held beliefs would judge the situation differently. The way you perceive the things would clearly reflect in the way you judge the things.

If I perceive the poor people as thieves, I would be judging the poor people as thieves. If I perceive a certain community as immoral, then I would be judging all the people of the community as immoral. Likewise, if I perceive the women wearing make-up and dressed in fashionable clothes as indecent, I would be judging women with make-up as the immoral.

The truth has got nothing to do with what one believes. I may believe that I am the most beautiful woman on this earth. It is my truth. But, it may or may not be the truth in the end. In the end, your truth is going to affect you. Likewise, people believe that their children are the world's best children. The statement may not be true. Truth has got nothing to do with what you believe.

Another point to be taken into the consideration is that no matter what you believe, everything is good, till it remains your belief alone. The moment you try to force your belief onto others, it is definitely a wrong thing on your part. I may believe that my religion is the world's best religion. It is my truth. But, if I am forcing others to convert to my religion because it is the best religion, it is definitely wrong thing on my part.

Forcing your truth on to other people is wrong. If you are free to practice your beliefs, so are others, free to practice their beliefs. Loving your religion is a good thing, but hating other religion is definitely not a good thing. If you are practicing vegetarianism, have tolerance for those practicing non-vegetarianism.

If you are following a certain dress code, show tolerance for those not abiding by it. Again, if you are fasting on certain days, extend your tolerance for those who are not. In fact, there is no need to force your views. After all, different people would define the same truth differently. The supreme truth remains unaffected, unchanged and unperturbed. The supreme truth cannot be diluted by anyone's beliefs or judgments. It's all up to you whether you accept the greater truths of life or not. If you are choosing a certain belief, irrespective of the truth, you have to face the consequence that comes from holding on to that belief. Nothing can be done against it.

No religion teaches to force your views onto others. No religion teaches intolerance. Still, we choose hatred over love, intolerance over tolerance, and enmity over brotherhood. The greater truth prevails. You cannot just murder someone and get away with it. No matter how many justifications you produce, wrong is still wrong.

If you have done something with wrong intent, no person on earth can save you from its consequences. And if you have not done anything wrong, you need not run after any one to get saved. Your truth alone is enough to save you. The whole point is to not hurt any living being intentionally. The greatest service is to not to hurt any living being. You should never hurt anybody, man, woman, children, animals, and even plants. It is the true religion. It is the supreme truth.

*The whole concept is to help others. And if you cannot do that, please don't hurt any living being. -Dalai Lama.*

# *HOW PARENTS JUDGED YOU*

## Your first teacher

*Parents are said to be child's first teachers.* Whatever things a child experiences in his early years stays forever. The emotional being of a child is greatly affected by the surroundings. It's imperative that growth should occur on all levels - physical, mental, social, and emotional levels. Because a child doesn't have an independent thinking of his own, the child absorbs everything in the environment and believes it to be true. Knowingly or unknowingly, parents teach so many things to a child. According to the parent's experiences they teach their children. The parents, the atmosphere, and the circumstances, play a big role in molding a child. Like the dry clay, the child absorbs everything. If a wrong impression is imbibed on his innocent mind, it is almost difficult to change it at a later stage.

## The impact

Whether right or wrong, the early impression remains with the child forever. The neighborhood, the school, and the outer world, impact a child's growth tremendously. You cannot be present everywhere to monitor how the outer world is affecting your child. The child may behave normally at home but may behave poorly outside. On the contrary, the child may behave poorly at home and may behave nicely outside. We can control our child's behavior in a tightly closed environment, but we cannot control his behavior in the outside environment. When certain things are beyond our control, it's imperative that we teach a child some indispensable lessons of life. It is the reason why it's so important that a child grows in the right environment with the right kind of people. It's because at the later stage it becomes almost difficult to change the impressions that may have been imbibed on the child's consciousness.

Parents project themselves through their children. Their thinking, feelings, beliefs, attitudes, and judgments are all projected through their children. Parents who themselves rarely tell lie, their children also seem to speak the truth. The parents, who have respect for the women, have their children respecting women in their later lives. A parent, who is involved in domestic violence, hurls abuses, and quarrels, will have his children doing the same. For the same reason, it is said that the parents should never fight with each other in front of their children, because it causes a negative impact on the child's mind. The innocent mind absorbs everything like a dry sponge, be it wrong or right. Whatever the child learns through the parents is often hard wired in the child's mind. At the later stage, it's very difficult to change the negative teachings and its negative effects.

## The parents' role

Parents play a crucial role in deciding the school; the child has to go. Sometimes, parents decide the hours of tuitions for the child? The college is decided by the parents, in some cases. The career is also decided by the parents, in some cases. Whether the child really likes the subject, matters little. It has been my general observation that in some homes, too much emphasis is given to become a good child. Being well behaved matters more than being curious or creative. Often, children who ask a lot of questions and are curious about things are discouraged. More emphasis is being laid for producing results than wasting precious amount of time in asking questions.

Often, children are judged by how well they excel in their examinations. Earning good grades becomes an indicator of a good student. How much you score is more important than how better you understand a subject. Children who score poorly are often ridiculed everywhere. Scoring good grades matter more than creativity.

Often, the lesser known creative fields like pottery or sculpting are discouraged for widely-known fields like medicine or engineering. The well-known roads that lead to success are encouraged. The little-known roads are often discouraged. The child's behavior is modified to such an extent that child forgets to live in his natural self. Too much emphasis is given on behaving well. This leads to lack of interest, loss of self-esteem, and loss of the creative self in the children. I have seen a lot of homes where a great amount of emphasis is being laid in getting good grades than in making the child actually understand the subject. In the short term, we may be happy by modifying the behavior of a child in a way that it fits into our definition of good. But, in the long term, it will hamper the overall wellness of the child.

## How would you judge this?

*Be a good girl or boy.*
*Good children don't cry like this.*
*Good children don't demand like this.*
*Good children never behave in this way.*
*Why don't you behave like a good child?*

*Do you want to be known as a bad child?*

*Our neighbor children are so well-behaved. Why can't you be like them?*

## The judgment begins early

Some parents put too much pressure on the child to excel in the exams. They are extremely interested in proving that their children are the best children, and they are among the best parent. There is too much pressure on a child to excel in all the fields, whether it is academics, sports, or the extracurricular activities. There are some cases where the child has been so exhausted physically, mentally, and emotionally, sometimes a medical intervention is needed. The worst thing to do is to compare one child with the other child. It's like comparing oranges to apples. Is there any need to do it?

Imagine what would happen if all the children become doctors or engineers? Don't we need artists, musicians, actors, and singers? Can we do without them? Most parents give more importance to good grades than to creativity. The worst kind of comparison is – *'if others can do it, why can't you?'* Every child is different, with different talents. Some are good at academics while some are good at sports. What comes naturally to you is your best bet. Still, parents intend to turn the academician in to a sport person. Is doing this justified?

## How would you judge this?

*If others can do it, why can't you?*
*Do you want to be left behind others?*
*Why are you lagging behind?*
*What is your problem?*
*Why can't you be normal like the other students?*

*Why don't you apply your head?*
*You are an embarrassment.*

## The mounting pressure within

Undue comparison leads too much pressure on a child. The general notion of linking grades to intelligence leads a child to desperately run after good grades. The child puts all his physical and mental resources in to studies. Even after putting all the efforts, if a child is unable to meet up the parent's expectations, the child is labeled as good-for-nothing. If a child is inclined towards sports or extracurricular activities, we discourage them to continue it. Technically speaking, good grades alone are not enough to land you a good job or a better salary. There is a lot more needed. It is better try to aim for expertise in whatever you try to do. It would go a really long way to realize the dreams.

## How would you judge this?

*Others can do it. Why can't you?*
*Look at others and try to be like them.*
*Others would surpass you.*
*Why you always lag behind others?*
*Why can't you be like others?*
*Others are better than you in every single aspect.*
*Your friends would move on to the next class.*
*You would remain stuck in the same class.*

## The neighbor next door

When it comes to comparing how good you are, who else is a better contender than you own neighbor? What does our neighbor eat, drink, think, feel, and act is a matter of great concern to us. We are too interested in what our neighbor does. Some people follow their neighbors to choose a restaurant, a gym, a spa, a shop, at a theatre so on and so forth. Then they exactly teach their children to follow the same pattern. They teach their children to outperform the other students. They teach their children to stay ahead of others. They teach them to follow others.

In other words, the *yardstick* for the excellence is the other people. For many parents the yardstick for excellence is how well their children excel in studies as compared to the other children. These parents frequently compare their children with others, be it studies, sports, or the extra-curricular activities. They never encourage the children to follow themselves. Everything revolves around following the other children.

A student may earn good grades without actually understanding the subject in depth. So, just securing good grades is no indicator that a student understands the subject well. Results matter more than the actual understanding. Lesser known jobs and career are often being discouraged for the well-known and more lucrative careers. Well-known roads that lead to success matter more than the lesser known roads.

Parents themselves should play a pro-active role in molding their child's creativity.

## How would you judge this?

*Look at our neighbor children; they are a lot better than you.*

*Our neighbor children are always well behaved. Why don't you be like them?*

*You would be left behind. Our neighbor children would move ahead.*

*Try to be like others. Others are a way ahead of you.*

## The shaming method

Some parents resort to the unacceptable practice of criticizing their own child in front of everybody. This method is the worst of all kind as it leaves an indelible impact on the child's mind forever. Even after becoming an adult, the child remembers the pain. It leaves an emotional scar on the young minds. Only time can tell how much it would take to heal such a wound. It's the physical wound that gets immediate attention. It's the emotional wound that often goes unnoticed. Unlike physical wounds, the emotional wounds take longer time to heal. Many times it happens that the emotional wounds are deeply embedded in the subconscious. These wounds take time to surface or erupt. Often, the person is unaware that the wound is present. If left untreated, these emotional wounds often grow in magnitude. These wounds interrupt a person's physical, mental, emotional, spiritual, and social growth.

## How would you judge this?

*You would never pass.*
*You are a waste of our money.*
*You would fail and be left behind.*
*Nothing goes into your head.*
*What's your problem?*
*You don't understand anything.*
*Nothing works for you.*
*You would bring us shame.*

## The punishment strategy

Unlike emotional wounds, the physical wounds are comparatively easy to heal. Of course, there is no denying the fact that wounds whether physical or mental leave an indelible impression on the mind. It's an established fact that corporal punishments only lead to poorer performances in the class. Parents think that corporal punishment would instill a sense of fear in the child's mind, and he would begin to take studies seriously. But things may not always go as anticipated. It's a fact that the happier a child is; the easier it is for him to learn things. A child cannot be forced to learn something. Even if we apply force, it would only work to an extent. Beyond a certain point, things return to their place as they existed before. It's clear that punishment strategy doesn't always works. It is only when a child really enjoys while learning, he learns quicker. Studies should be a matter of enjoyment which comes naturally and should never be a burden.

## The bribing method

We all did it, at least at some point in our lives, bribing our own children. We say to a child that if he performs well in an examination, we will give him something good. And guess what? This method actually works. The child begins to put all his efforts hoping to get his favorite thing. In the short term, employing this method is not bad. But in the long term, this method is not advisable. The reason is the child gets addicted to the end-result. The greed starts growing. It's here the real problem begins. The child becomes too demanding. The problem augments when left unchecked. In the end, it would lead to results we did not anticipate.

*If you pass, I would take you to amusement park.*
*If you do this, I would buy you your favorite candy.*
*If you get good grades, we would be holidaying there.*
*I will take you to your favorite store if you do this.*
*I will buy you an expensive toy if you score well in the exams.*

## The empathic parents

Some parents really understand their kids well and encourage their kids to take the road less travelled. If their child wants to be a geologist or a pottery maker, they readily agree. They never give an advice unless asked for. That doesn't mean that they are a negligent parent. The thing is, they are watchful but only interrupt when it's really needed. The parent-child relationship, in this case, is the strongest of all. Since a child has nothing to hide, the parents become more of a friend. There are very few parents who would encourage their children to follow their heart. It takes courage to per sue the offbeat careers. It's when people around you understand you; it becomes a lot easier to follow your dreams. The more understanding between the parents and children, the stronger the bond of trust is developed.

Whether it's choosing a career, or decision to quit an unfulfilling job, or decision to marry a girl - parents rarely give prompt consent. In fact, from the very beginning itself, the child should be encouraged to pursue what he or she loves doing the most. Whether it's going for an offbeat career, choosing a less lucrative profession, or quitting a demanding job, it's always best for parents to whole heartedly accept child's decision. While it would be difficult for you to accept the fact that your only son wants to get married to girl of his own choice. It would be harder for your son who knows that he has to go ahead despite your disapproval. No matter how unconventional it may sound, being a geologist may prove more satisfying for your child. Even if you don't like it, sometimes it's better to agree for the benefit of your child.

## How would you judge this?

*You should do what you like the most.*
*You should outperform yourself.*

*Follow yourself. Stop chasing others.*
*Even if you fail, I will be there for you.*
*No matter what your grades, I would be with you.*
*You can choose an offbeat career if you are really interested.*

## The worst affected

Children of the broken homes are the hardest hit in parents fight. Unable to cope up with tough times, the child may become vulnerable to drugs, alcohol, or substance abuse. More than blaming the child for his poor behavior, the parents should be blamed. Only a deep introspection would help realize the gravity of the problem. If you don't introspect, who else will? If you, yourself don't look after your child, who else will? What is inside will be reflected at the outside. It's that simple.

The more emphasis on the good qualities, the more it would reflect on the outside. When a person gets too angry on the trivial issues, we say that the person has got parent's traits. When we find a child stealing something, we say that his parents didn't provide him good values. Likewise, we see a child hurling abuses at his fellow mates; we immediately say that his parents didn't teach the good things.

The emotions of the parents are fully absorbed by the child, whether good or bad, positive or negative. When so much of energy, traits, and the behavioral pattern are absorbed by a child, the parents should make sure that their child absorbs their positive energy and not the negative ones. The blame for the child's faulty behavior goes on to the parents. The parents' way of thinking, feeling, and doing the things is sometimes observed in the child. The child behaves in a particular manner too. Consciously or unconsciously, you are always projecting yourself through your children. A happy child is an adult of tomorrow. Every child is a valuable asset to the nation.

# *HOW TEACHERS JUDGE YOU*

## Your second home

School is said to be a child's second home. Whatever a child learns from the school stays forever with the child. Like a plant that can thrive only in correct environment with proper sunlight, air, water, and fertilizer for the growth; the same holds true for the child. A child who gets right environment, proper guidance, the right exposure, and the timely intervention to introspect will surely blossom. Then a child turns into a good human being. Learning should be a joyous process. It should never be a burden. I have personally believed that learning that comes from textbooks is the half truth. The eternal truths of life, the common sense, and the life experiences, are not taught in the textbooks. These are the truths that are the essence of life and which everybody has to deal with in their lives.

A body is said to be in good health when it's all body parts work in a total harmony. If any part of the body is neglected, then the overall health is affected. A harmonious balance between all the body parts is a healthy body. Likewise, a school should be a harmonious balance of studies, sports, social interactions, and extracurricular activities. It helps a child achieve growth in every field. A delicate balance between too much and too little of a thing should be maintained. Equal emphasis should to given to the textbook curriculum and gaining practical knowledge.

Gaining practical knowledge is as necessary as the theoretical knowledge. The student becomes more confident in facing the *'real-life'* related problems. In this way, the general being of the student is safe-guarded. It's imperative that equal emphasis should be given to all aspects of life. Along with the textbooks, equal importance should also be given to the other activities like sports, social skills, and healthy communication. Care should be taken that growth happens at all the levels – physical, mental, emotional, and spiritual.

A proper development of the student is possible only when there is an equal amount of emphasis to all fields. No area should be over emphasized. Good grades shouldn't be gained at the cost of health or mental peace. My own personal experience says that too much importance is given to scoring good grades in academics. Creativity can only flourish in an encouraging environment. Too much emphasis on the theoretical knowledge only hampers the creativity of a child. If a student scores well, then he is said to be a good student. If he doesn't, then he is a bad student. The greatest disadvantage of the grading system is that it becomes the only yardstick for measuring student's success. If you succeed, then you are a good student. If you don't, then you are a bad student. These grades are test of your memory only. It doesn't show how much of a creative intelligence a student possesses. In the end, the grading system of the school is to be blamed for emphasizing too much on good grades.

Holding the teachers responsible for everything is a total injustice.

## How would you judge this?

If a child doesn't perform well at school everybody right from the parents, the teachers, and the elders come into immediate action. The study hours are extended, the playing periods are shortened, the external distractions are cut off, and the social ties are reduced. Parents jump into the scene by personally inspecting everything. Teachers ensure that the child is concentrating properly. The elders ensure that there are no distractions around. In other words, everybody puts their best to craft out a good student. If the desired results aren't achieved in spite of following all the desperate measures, the child is blamed from all the quarters. The child is labeled as lazy, dull, and a good-for-nothing.

Everyone becomes so distraught with the poor performance; as if the child has no future at all. We immediately jump to the conclusion that the child is not working hard enough. The child feels guilty for not being able to match up to the expectations. The joy of learning turns into the burden of learning. The pressure to excel takes its toll on health, self-esteem, communication levels, and the social presence of the child. If a student cannot relate the things taught in textbooks to real life, then it's a huge disappointment. Students are punished for not scoring good grades. They end up their lives for being unable to match up to the expectations of their elders.

## How would you judge this?

Children cannot differentiate between the right and the wrong. It's our collective responsibility to ensure that a child is being taken care of. Growth should occur at all the levels – physical, mental, emotional, and spiritual. Everybody should be given a fair chance to flourish. Right from the school days, one thing that I have personally experienced is that too much emphasis is given on good grades. Right from the parents, the teachers, the elders, and almost everyone strives hard to help a child achieve good grades. The yardstick for excellence is good grades. If you excelled in academics, then you are being labeled as a good student. If you couldn't, then you are labeled as a not-so-good student.

## How would you judge this?

*You are a good student.*
*You would make us proud.*
*You are a genius.*
*You have a great potential.*
*You would do something great.*
*All our hopes rest on you.*
*You would never let us down.*

## How would you judge this?

Parents invest a considerable amount of energy to make their children bright students. Teachers spend an enormous amount of energy to bring out the best of a student. And finally, students invest a lot of energy in proving that they are the best students. Everyone including the parents, the elders, and the teachers join hands together to help the child become a good student. In fact, everybody is trying to do their best. When it comes to the not-so-bright students, the case is entirely different. Rigorous study plans, tight schedules, long hours of daily practice, and the tuitions are the standard procedures followed. Everybody is on a mission. The teachers alone cannot be held responsible for everything. The grading system of the school leads to a mounting pressure on the students.

Parents have to prove that their children are the best. Teachers have to prove that their students are the best. Again, children have to prove that they are the best students. The poor students have to pump in all their energy to score good grades. The desperation can be clearly seen on their faces, from attending the school, the tuitions and the extra classes, and turning to the almighty desperately for the help, every possible method is tried. Nothing is left to chance. All this hard work is done to improve the grades.

## How would you judge this?

*If others can do it, why can't you?*

I have experienced that often the parents, the elders, the teachers, and the people around the student, often compare one student to the other student. Undue comparison creates bad impression on the child. It's like comparing *an orange to an apple*. Each one has its own unique identity and its own distinct characteristics. You just cannot compare the two. Every child is unique, different, and wonderful. You cannot make all the students fit into the same mold. Someone is good at mathematics. Other is good at literature. Actually there is no comparison between any two. No one is above. No one is beneath.

One would become an engineer; the other would become a creative writer. How can there be a comparison between the two? Both of them are equally needed for proper functioning of life. Why is the comparison? Why the loss of energy into making an orange into an apple? Can't we accept ourselves just the way we are? Why do we need to change somebody? Is it not wonderful that each one of is completely unique? Why can't we accept the differences?

What would happen if everybody wants to be a great mathematician or a great scientist? Can we continue to live in a world full of mathematicians and scientists alone? Don't we need doctors, engineers, painters, cleaners, electricians, housemaids, milkman, and the mail carrier? Could you think of existing without them? Is life the same without them? If they are not so important in our lives, why is that we can't live without them. In the competition to earn good grades, the joy of learning takes backseat.

Learning shouldn't be just confined to the four walls of the classroom. It should be extended to all spheres of life. Whoever teaches you, is a teacher, whether it's your grandpa teaching you mathematics, your neighbor aunt teaching you the basics of good health, or your neighbor's daughter teaching you how to draw. Everybody who has contributed in teaching you something is a teacher. That's the secret to being a good learner. Learning should be a joyous process rather than a burdensome process.

## How would you judge this?

*They can do it. Why can't you?*
*You should be ahead of others.*
*Look at others and learn from them? You shouldn't let others to surpass you.*
*Look at others and be ahead of them.*

## The act of kindness

I fondly remember one of my school teachers who convinced a parent. The student wanted to pursue an off-beat career, but his parents were insisting on medical or engineering. The teacher understood the student's dilemma and convinced the parents. The student is now a happily employed geologist in a renowned company. I remember a day when one of my teachers shared her lunch-box with me as I had forgotten to bring mine. This teacher would always share her lunch with anyone who forgot to bring his lunch box. These acts of kindness stay forever.

## Life is the greatest teacher

Along with the textbook knowledge, the life's lessons are equally important. Compassion, forgiveness, humility, brotherhood, and peace would always rule the world. It's imperative that the child becomes a good human being as well. If you are scoring good grades but are unable to attend to your wounded pet, your education is incomplete. Textbook lessons should not only be confined to textbooks alone, but it should be extended to the real life as well. Only then you are said to be educated, when you have applied the knowledge in all the fields of life. When everybody including you has been benefitted with your education, only then you are said to be completely educated. And only those are liberated who have applied knowledge in helping out themself and others alike. Life's lessons should be understood. Compassion, forgiveness, humility, brotherhood, and peace should also be taught along with the text book syllabus. What's the use of education if it can't make us human? There are many people who are highly educated; still they lack the basic virtues like compassion, forgiveness, and humility. They think just because they are highly trained, they can look down upon others.

## Learning is a life-long process

A mail carrier may not be highly educated, but he may display high levels of compassion whereas a highly paid CEO may show his poor side by displaying arrogance. Whom do you think is more compassionate of the two? In the end, it's the love we shared and the love we received is all that matter. Isn't it?

*A good teacher never stops teaching. A good student never stops learning. That's how the good people are. They consistently keep on improving themselves.*

You cannot say at any point that, yes, this is it, now I won't have to learn anymore, do anything, or work anymore. If you want to excel in any field, you need to improve yourself continuously, and you have to be a better person today than you were yesterday. You have to put in a little more of your heart than you did yesterday. How could tomorrow be better, if your today isn't better? Nothing will change unless you want to change. For a better tomorrow, you have to work hard today. There is absolutely no substitution to hard work. A good learner never stops learning. He keeps on improving himself. Learning is a life-long process. It should not be confined to four walls of the classroom.

## The real life experiences

Unless you learn from your own real life experiences, you won't be able to meet the ever-changing challenges of life. It's the direct experience that comes from the real life that matters. You cannot keep the children isolated from the rest of the world and expect them to be just a book worm. If we expect the student to excel in every field, we need to ensure that the student gets proper guidance and the right exposure. Timely motivation brings excellent results. My own experience says that everybody including the parents, the teachers, and the elders should help a child. A child should become more aware of his surroundings, circumstances, and the people around him. Sadly, this doesn't always happen. Blaming the teacher alone for this situation is certainly injustice. The school grade system, the authorities, and the government, in general, should have a deep introspection about the negative consequences of the school grading system. A child is not just a child. He is an asset to a nation. It's our collective responsibility to ensure that our future generations are provided with the best care and facilities.

# *HOW SIBLINGS JUDGE EACH OTHER*

## The heart to heart connection

Unlike the parents or the elders, who have an authoritative control over us, siblings are more or less the alike. They know every single detail about us, our likes, dislikes, the first crush, the first heart break, the best friends, the favorite pastime, the favorite coffee destination, and the favorite cloth brand. The things we would usually surf on the internet, they know everything about it. It has been found that either there is a good understanding between the siblings or there isn't any connection at all.

## My sister

I would like to cite an example of my sister. I have a younger sister. I don't know why I was never close to my parents. It was my sister who understood me. She meant everything to me. We bonded really well. In fact, both of us would understand each other very well. We would share all the pain and all the joys together. The bonding grew strong over the years. What others could never understand, my little sister could. She could easily understand the silent tears, the silent joy, the silent pain; everything that was unsaid. I could share almost everything, without the fear of being judged or misunderstood. Thankfully, there was someone who understood me and always stood by me during the tough times.

## Siblings share a strong bond

When it comes to siblings, either there is a supportive and friendly relation or there is envy and jealousy. Siblings can be more of a friend. Like, friends, they know everything about us and still love us. Siblings help us to unlock our true potential. They may even help to understand our deepest desires. Whether it's a school project, or choosing a dress at a shopping mall, nobody other than the sibling can help you better in accomplishing these tasks. Whether you are being scolded by your parents for eating your favorite ice-cream behind the doors, or you have reached home late, the only person who can help you is your sibling.

They help you overcome almost any situation. They are friends with blood ties. They encourage us to achieve the best we can. You can share the problems that you may find it difficult to share with your parents. Since they are of the same age, they understand us really well. It's the bond of love that helps us sail through the turbulent times. A sibling can bring the best in each other.

Sometimes, we don't know ourselves what we really want; siblings could play their role in finding out the best in you. They can show how to perform well in the exam. They know exactly that literature is your favorite subject and mathematics is your weak point. When somebody knows your strengths and weaknesses thoroughly, they will correctly guide you to your true potential. Most of the siblings often get along with each other very well. They know you to the core. The hidden emotions are often interpreted correctly by the siblings. Siblings understand what you are feeling and what you are trying to hide.

The time spent together, the mischievousness done together, the laughter, and the petty fights stays with the siblings forever. Fighting over the larger share of cake, blaming each other after a flower vase is broken, confessing guilty to save the other from being punished, these little moments spent and sacrifices done stays forever. The love and sacrifices that is often found in the siblings is often life-long. Siblings can even sacrifice their lives to save each other.

## How would you judge this?

*You are good at this.*
*You should try these colors.*
*You should learn in this way.*
*You should be friendly.*
*He's, or she's cheating on you.*

## The total contrast

On the contrary, it has been found that some sibling don't get together well. They often fight with each other voraciously, have issues, and their lot of time is wasted in teaching each other a lesson. Whatever the reason, the precious time spent to put each other down could have been used to help one another. But this doesn't always happen. Apart from being incompatible with each other, they fight on issues that are trivial. Often, fights may begin with a small issue and soon turn into a big fight. No matter how much you try to make them understand, they choose to shut down their eyes. No amount of advice helps them become friendly. These fights often lead to an emotional wound that may fade away with time, but the scars remains.

A deep down jealously, too much of interference with each other, fighting over petty things, ego problems, lack of mutual respect, lack of faith in one another, and a complete lack of understanding are ingredients that can easily shake any relationship. Often, these relationships fail the test of time.

A healthy communication and more investment of time in understanding each other is the key to a happier and stable relationship. It has been found that in the fight to win their parent's love; the siblings try to put each other down. Everything comes down to just one thing, to get noticed and to earn love.

In the pursuit to earn love, often siblings can go to any extent. Undue parental love showered upon one child leads to such things. The parents should be blamed for such gross negligence. Parents favoring the one child and neglecting the other, often gives rise to hatred, jealousy and competition in the siblings. If left unchecked, this tendency leads to disastrous results later on.

Too much competition and jealousy can wreck a relationship. Only love and understanding can counter these negativities. Mutual respect and love can help the siblings understand each other. Instead of crossing each other's path for the wrong reason, they should try to help each other. Love begets love. Whatever you give will ultimately come back to you. So, instead of choosing hatred and enmity, it's better to choose love and understanding for each other. Love wins everybody. It's the love that remains in the end.

## How would you judge this?

*You are a loser.*
*Nothing works for you.*
*You are a complete idiot.*
*You are an embarrassment.*
*What's wrong with you?*
*You will end up as a failure.*

# *HOW NEIGHBORS JUDGE YOU*

### They know everything

Our beloved neighbors know almost every single detail about us. Some neighbors exactly know our waking time for jogging, the things we have for breakfast, our daily routine of work, the company where we have been employed, the school where our children go to, and our favorite restaurant, our neighbor probably know everything about us.

They know every single thing in detail.

Nobody knows us better than our own neighbors. They know things to such a point that you sometimes feel threatened. From where we had been, to where we would like to, neighbors know every detail with high level of accuracy. Like a mirror, they almost reflect every single thing about us. It's sometimes frustrating to know that people are more interested in knowing others than knowing themselves. It's strange that people are not that much interested in themselves as they are in others. It's weird that some neighbors are overly curious in knowing every single detail about us.

Whether it is your children's school, the college, or the office, neighbors know every single thing about you whether it is a petty thing or a major one. They are the ones who sometimes know us better than we know ourselves.

If your son is single and unmarried, people want to know the reasons for it. If your son is married, people want to know the reasons for not having kids. If your son is married and have kids, then people want to know something else.

Whether you are single, married, or divorcee, some people are always curious to know about you.

## How would you judge this?

*How are your child's studies going on?*
*Did your son have a love marriage?*
*Why is your son single?*
*Is everything alright?*

## Know thyself

In the bible there is a beautiful saying – *know thyself*. What does it mean to know ourselves? Why are we being asked to know ourselves? Don't we understand ourselves enough? The answer is no; we never try to know ourselves. The time and effort we spent on knowing others can be spent in knowing ourselves. It's strange that we find out more about the school of our neighbor's child than we know about our own children. Likewise, it's weird too, that we know every detail about our neighbor's workplace than we actually know about our own. We find out more about others than we should. We invest a large deal of our time, energy, and efforts in understanding others than we spend into knowing ourselves. What others do should be more of others' business than ours.

## We too, follow our neighbor

If our neighbor goes to a particular restaurant for food, we want to check that place for ourselves. If our neighbor goes to a particular gym, we want to check it out ourselves. Likewise, if our neighbor visits a particular doctor, we too rush to that doctor for the treatment. Why is this so? We form a connection between what our neighbor likes and what is excellence.

We create an impression that our neighbor's choice has to be good. The cloth brand, the shopping mall, the dentist, the grocery store, or the choice of music, if our neighbor has chosen these things, then it's got to be good. We never doubt about it. We tend to forget what our own likes and dislikes. We immediately jump into conclusion that our neighbor's choice has to be good. But generally speaking, what is good for the others may not be good for you.

In other words, what works for others may not work for you. If your neighbor has lost a lot of weight by practicing certain exercises, then it doesn't mean that you would be able to do the same. It would be no short than harming ourselves. If your neighbor has lost 45 lbs of weight in few months, then it doesn't mean you would be able to do exactly the same.

We want to be ahead of our neighbor, and we, in turn, teach our children to follow the same. We teach our children to always be ahead of the other students. The only test to know if our child is doing well in the exam is whether he has scored better than the other students or not. We constantly compare our children with the other children. If our child is ahead of other children on all the parameters, we become happy. If other children are ahead in the race and our child are lagging behind, we become sad. The *yardstick* for measuring excellence is the other people. The yardsticks for measuring our children's excellence are the other children. In other words, the yardstick for measuring excellence is other people. In fact, it should be our endeavor to be a better person today than what we were yesterday. Instead, we jump into a never ending vicious cycle trying to prove that we are the best. Nobody gets benefited by this way.

All the precious energy is utilized into things that don't matter much. There is absolutely nothing wrong in knowing others. Being curious is human nature. To understand others, so that we can know them better is a good thing. But being overly curious and forgetting ourselves is not a good thing. We shouldn't forget ourselves in the quest to understand others. If we find something good in others, we should try to inoculate those good things in ourselves. Likewise, when we see something bad in others, we should strive to change that in us too. There's no point in passively seeing things and not attempting to change it. Things must be changed for better. You should be changed for better.

## How do you judge this?

We are social beings. It's imperative that we should be attentive to our surroundings. Due to urbanization, modernization, and the quest to earn more money, people are living in nuclear families. We have become so closed in our own shells that we often don't know the name of our neighbor living adjacent to us. We don't care to see whether they are in a happy state or not. If we call this modernization, contemplate where are we heading towards?

We don't know whether our neighbor is healthy or ill. We don't know whether our neighbor is in some sort of problem. We don't know if they need our help. Is this what we call a civilization, where a person doesn't even know the name of the person living just nearby? Due to modernization, a person is left alone in the midst of trouble to fend himself. In this busy life, everyone is busy in one's own world. Is it not our duty to help our own neighbor if he is in midst of difficulties? The most painful thing is that, often, we are not in talking terms to our neighbors. We don't care a bit. Everybody is lost in their own world of business.

## The missing factor

We don't know our neighbor's names, their difficulties, their joys, and their pains. We know nothing about them. We have become so modern that we have become lonely and abandoned. The parent to children communication has been severely affected. The communication with our neighbor has been cut down. We communicate less and fight more. We don't have someone to share our feelings, emotions, joy, and pain. We all are struggling with our loneliness. Each one of us is fighting a silent fight.

Communication between family, friends, and people has been restricted to hi and hello. The short message services have replaced the heart to heart chat. The hours of chatting together, the weekend trips, the fun together, everything is lost. Everyone is being confined to the four walls. People don't have time for their family, friends, neighbors, and other people around them. People don't have time for each other. People don't have time for themselves either.

People eat in a hurry, walk in a hurry, and talk in a hurry. One should understand more and judge less. The best thing is to put in all the energy to know ourselves better. The more preoccupied we are with the outer world, the less time we would get to know ourselves. The best thing to do is to start knowing ourselves, little by little every day. The more we know ourselves, the better it is for us. We never try to see the complete picture. Just by seeing the half picture, we jump to the conclusions. We understand less, but judge more. In fact, we should be more understanding and judging less, but this never happens. The world needs fewer people who judgmental. The world needs more people who understand; People those are emphatic and sensitive towards each other.

# *HOW FRIENDS JUDGE YOU*

## The true friend

There are blood relations; and there are other relations that are stronger than the blood relations. Friendship is one of those relations. We think that a family is someone with a blood relation. But this is not the whole truth. Anyone who is there to help you in the adverse times is a family. A friend, a Samaritan, a helping neighbor, or a compassionate passerby, all one of them is family. It has been found that during the growing stages of life, children are more close to their friends than they are with their parents. This bond of trust and mutual respect often continues to the adulthood. You can share almost anything with friends. The things that cannot be shared with others can be shared with friends. No matter what the situation is, a true friend is always there to help.

Whether it's choosing the color of a dress, the dilemma over career, or a major problem confronted in life, your friends always have a solution. Real friends have a solution to almost every problem of yours. They are someone you can always lean on. Whether it's an evening spent together, a surprise birthday party, or a relaxing weekend, true friends make the difference.

Real friends don't judge each other. They complement each other. True friends' help each other grow. They help you in every possible way, and they support you in midst of all adversities. They know almost every single thing about you. They know your favorite restaurant, the things that upset you, and the things that lighten up your face, your beliefs, the good and bad things about you, your crushes, your strengths, your weaknesses, and your fears, true friends possibly know everything about you.

Some friends would happily sacrifice their lives for a friend. They know exactly what makes you happy. True friends know every little thing about you, your favorite ice-cream flavor, the favorite café, the favorite cloth brand, or the best shoe brand. From the trivial to the most serious issues, true friends are ever ready to help.

From getting the best counselor in the city, helping you financially in the midst of crisis, or becoming a mediator in a quarrel, true friends are certainly there for you. They advise you curtly without fearing the consequences. They can tell you that a particular dress doesn't suit you. They can tell you to leave a job that you don't like. They can influence you to become a strong man or woman so that peoples' opinion seldom perturbs you. They don't mind telling you the truth for your betterment. Even if it's hurting, some truths shouldn't be over looked.

True friends help you realize these truths. True friends make you realize how important it is to take proper care of yourselves; they would ask you to change a dress if it's looking awkward and they would advise you to cut on to the fat intake to help you stay healthy. If you are into a relationship and if it's not working, you should reveal it to a friend. True friends always do this.

True friends know all about you right from the minute details to larger ones.

## How would you judge this?

*You should do this way.*
*You should eat these foods.*
*It is so your color.*
*You should open up.*
*I am always there for you.*

## How you judge this?

Not always you find that everybody is supportive. There are unsupportive friends too. They bully you, make fun of you, and put you down. There are only two reasons why people laugh at you, either you are way ahead of them or you are trailing them in the race of the life. Whether you wore a beautiful dress, you gave the best presentation ever, or you were being promoted for your hard work, there would always be a bunch of friends who wouldn't be impressed at all.

No matter what you achieve, some would always talk behind your back. Jealousy, hatred, and ego blinds these friends completely. They find it hard to accept your goodness. They hate you for no reason. They put you down despite your good intentions. No amount of good will, forgiveness, and loving intentions work with these people. The only way to move on is to forgive them completely and stay focused on your job. No circumstances, no person, absolutely nothing can rob you of your mental peace unless you permit them to do so.

Whether it's a bad friend at the school, at the college, or at the job, you cannot avoid them. They often judge you; talk negatively about you and try to rupture your self-esteem. They are always around to see that you don't move ahead in your life. No matter how happy they are from within, nothing gives them more pleasure than to see you in pain. They never miss a point to tell your weaknesses to others. They hate you for no reason. The only thing that makes them happy is your failures and weaknesses. They are least interested in knowing themselves. All their efforts are utilized in knowing about you and your life.

When running away from them doesn't works, it is always better that you learn ways to deal with the problem. In willfully hurting others to teach them a lesson, we get hurt ourselves. In pulling someone down, we too crash.

We hurt someone hoping that we might never get hurt, but we do get. Nobody has ever escaped the consequences of the wrong deeds. Something which is done with intent to hurt someone is very likely to hurt you in the end.

## How would you judge this?

*You look awkward.*
*It is not your color.*
*You can never do this.*
*It's not your cup of tea.*
*Stop trying. You won't succeed.*

# *HOW LOVE INTEREST/SPOUSE JUDGE YOU*

## The love

It has been found that there is love between the couple or there is no love at all. The love interest or spouse is always judged on the romantic parameters, but this is always not the case. They can help you grow in the areas you never thought of including emotional and spiritual. We never think beyond the romantic alliance. We get accustomed to the thinking that the relationship with spouse has to be a romantic union.

In fact, there are many areas which can be explored like emotional, spiritual, and social. Couples either love too much or hate too much. Either love helps them explore their unknown sides or hate reveals their worst side. Couples who are in love help each other grow. These couples are of supportive, compassionate, and understanding nature. They know what is holding you back. They help you unlock your true potential. They know your strengths and weaknesses alike. They love you despite your limits. Couples in true love can help each other grow like no other can.

A genuinely loving couple would be quick in resolving their differences to lead a happy married life. If at all the differences arise, they work on those points together. A truly loving couple work together to make their marriage succeed, they eat together, they laugh together, and they cry together. A bond of togetherness is formed. It's not that these couples never have any differences or any fights. It's just that they are quick to resolve things and stay together.

It's their strong desire to be with each other that keeps them together. Lack of proper communication, lack of understanding, and lack of mutual respect for each other, often leads to the deterioration of a relationship. A successful marriage is often the result of a successful communication. These couples understand each other so well that they often understand the non-verbal gestures as easily as the verbal messages. It's the love, the proper communication, the good understanding, and the mutual self-respect that lead to a strong relation. They very well know each other's' weaknesses and turn them into strengths.

## How would you judge this?

*You look pretty in this color.*
*You look beautiful.*
*We look great together.*
*You are the best.*

## How do you judge this?

The love that is present at the earlier stage begins to fade. In order to make a good impression on others, people try to hide their real self, and over a period, the real self gets suppressed. In the quest to earn love, the fake person takes over. This is one of the reason that people don't find their love to be everlasting. Love transforms when people transform. What people used to be earlier, contradicts their present. The life after the marriage becomes boring, monotonous, and uninteresting.

Isn't it strange that the same people who were happy together in earlier stages find it dull and boring later on? It's as if something has been altered. What's the difference? As soon as one gets married, one finds the life churning. It becomes the same boring life, the same droning person, the same dull job, and the routine becomes monotonous. The same fights and the same arguments aggravate to the boredom.

## The love begins to fade

The unconditional love turns into demanding. The empathy turns into apathy; the willingness turns into reluctance, and acceptance turns into judgment.

The same person who earlier appeared to be interesting turns into a dull person, the loving person becomes unloving, the adorable becomes unadorable, the helpful becomes unhelpful, the active turns into gloomy, love turns into hate, and the cooperative turns into uncooperative.

People change. Things change. Priorities change.

People no longer find it interesting to dine together, to talk together, to work together, to laugh together, and the most importantly to love each other. People change so drastically that it is evident by the way they behave with each other. Love changes to hatred. They no longer remain supportive. Communication takes a backseat. When couples begin judging each other, every argument starts getting personal. Instead of helping each other grow, some couples begin to pull each other down. It is where the downfall in their marriages occurs.

Couples start fighting and judging each other and the result is a weaker relationship. A little understanding, a little sacrifice, and a little compassion can work wonders in love. We all need little of kindness. Less understanding weakens belief in each other. The less we understand ourselves, the more we distance ourselves from each other.

It's not the arguments or the conflicts that hurt us, but the way in which the words are being exchanged that gives the pain. A simple argument turns into a heated one. We neither understand ourselves nor others. We forget where to draw the line. We forget to respect each other's privacy. Too much closeness weakens a relationship.

Either there is love between the couples or there is no love at all. Couples who fight with each other for whatever reason put in all their energies into pulling each other down. They don't respect each other, talk to each other, and most importantly love each other. The love turns into hatred; empathy turns into apathy, understanding into indifference, and carefulness to carelessness, and sensitivity into insensitivity.

The people turn sour. The things turn sour. The marriage turns sour.

## How you judge this?

> You have gained weight.
> You should avoid these foods.
> Why the house can't be kept clean.
> Why the house is always untidy?
> Why did I marry you?
> *You are a fool.*
> *You are not beautiful.*
> *Why can't you do this?*
> *Why can't you do that?*
> *You are an embarrassment.*
> *You would end up as a failure.*

# *HOW GOD JUDGES YOU?*

### Killing the innocent in the name of god

There are some self-proclaimed righteous persons or groups who claim that their way of doing things is the only right way. They also claim that they never do anything wrong, and god loves them. They kill innocent people in the name of god and think that god would be pleased by their act; not knowing that the very same god would punish them for their acts.

Every person feels him or her to be the most important person in this world. But god doesn't think this way. For god, every single living being on the earth is as important as all. God loves everybody alike – man, women, children, plants, or the animals. God doesn't choose to play favorites among people. God loves everybody equally. Every life is sacred. Life should be respected. Every religion teaches that life is sacred, and no killing should be carried out in the name of god. Every religious text book has condemned the killing of innocent people.

*Killing the innocent lives in the name of religion is the highest form of god's disobedience.*

## The mould

There is no doubt about the fact that as a child, the surroundings we had to live in, has a tremendous impact on the way we would think, feel, and act in the later stages of life. It is natural that each one of us has been raised by believing that their faith and rituals are the correct way to lead a life. There is absolutely nothing wrong in thinking that our way of thinking is the best until we do not force our way of thinking on the others. Imagine what would happen when everyone would come together on a single platform thinking that their way of thinking is the best? There would definitely be a clash.

The whole world is one large family. There are different people, countries, religions, caste, creed, race, languages, the ways of eating, and the way of dressing, etc. Even the ways in which people greet are different in different religions. In some religions or countries, greeting is done with the folded hands while in other nations; it's a handshake. Every religion or country has its unique way of greeting someone. Also, people have various kinds of places of worship in different faiths. No matter what faith you practice, every faith is good if it is leading to god. Every way of doing things is good until we are not imposing that onto others.

In some religion, there are certain kinds of food which are considered acceptable for eating and there are certain kind of food which should be abstained from eating. Again, there are certain days that are considered sacred and it's during these days certain foods are strictly prohibited. Is it justified fighting over the eating issues?

Likewise, people can be seen fighting with each other for asserting their views and opinions. No matter what religion someone may practice, if a person has murdered somebody, he cannot escape just by belonging to a particular faith. Likewise, no matter how rich you are, you cannot escape punishment just because you are rich. The justice system of god in this world is above all the money, caste, creed, or age.

There is only one supreme truth that binds all the people and the religions of the world. That truth is that god loves each living being on this earth equally. God never chooses to love one person above the other. So, whether you are rich or poor, it doesn't matter to god. God loves you.

If you did nothing wrong, nobody can make you suffer. If you did something wrong, nobody can save you. It's our own karmas that can either save us or drown us. It is our own good karmas that lead to joy and our bad karmas that lead to pain. God never plays a judge to reward or punish people. Contrary to the popular belief, God never judges nor does play the role of a mediator between the people. God never ever punishes anybody. The concept of hell and heaven are man-made. It's our own karmas that eventually catch us up.

## How you judge this?

A person working in a cigarette producing factory would argue against banning cigarettes stating that he has a right to livelihood while the same product is a killer for others. In other words, the cigarette is a killer for some; for others, it is a means to livelihood. It can be easily established that the definition of morality differs from person to person. An individual who kills animals for livelihood may claim that he is only carrying out his job while other people may argue that he is taking an innocent life.

A person working in a factory that produces cracker and the other explosive items might argue that it's his livelihood, and others might claim that the products are harmful. It's clearly evident that that the definition of morality differs from person to person, and situation to situation.

So, how to judge who is right and who is wrong? The answer is simple. Use your own discretion in judging things. Many things in this world that is often contradictory to our own beliefs. What one may find right, the other may find wrong. What one thinks to be morally correct, the other may find wrong.

Take this example. No religion asks its followers to hurt any living being, still people kill each other. Later, people try to justify themselves saying that they carried the killings in the name of religion. It is clearly written in all the religious books to not hurt anyone; this is the supreme truth in its original form. But, we Hurt someone intentionally and later justify it in the name of religion, this is a modified truth. It is a modified truth because it is nowhere written in any religious book that one should hurt another.

We modify the truth for our own convenience.

What is right to someone may not be right to somebody else. It is very clear that different people would define the same truth differently. Though the people are free to define the truth according to their way of thinking, still, people are certainly not free to escape the consequences the modified truth brings along with it. In other words, you are free to accept the truth in its original form or to choose modified truth, but, in the end, you should be ready to accept the consequences. Escaping the aftermaths of the modified truth is hard.

By modifying the supreme truth for our own convenience, we are sure to head on a wrong path.

## The right, the wrong

According to the teachings we had been taught at the home, at the school, we all form certain following judgments.

*What is good and what is bad.*
*What is moral and what is immoral.*

*What should be eaten and what shouldn't be.*
*What should be worn and what shouldn't be?*
*What should be the means of livelihood?*
*What should be the code of the conduct?*
*What should be the reward and the punishment?*
*What should be accepted and what shouldn't be.*

There are certain things which come out clearly. Our early conditioning in the life plays a major role in determining our way of thinking in our later life. Each one of us has a different definition about morals, good and correct things. What one finds wrong; the other may finds right. What one finds immoral; the other finds immoral. In the end, different people define the same truth differently.

For instance, one religion advocates vegetarianism while another religion advocates non-vegetarianism. One religion asserts that women should wear clothes modestly while another religion allows women to dress liberally.

In some countries woman wearing clothes liberally is not seen as moral. Contrarily, a woman wearing clothes liberally is seen as moral in some countries. In few countries, some professions are held as not moral for the women. Contrarily, few professions are not taken into account bad for women in some countries.

In some countries, the guilty is publically prosecuted. Contrarily, the accused is given fair chance to defend oneself through a competent lawyer in other countries.

A person chooses to abstain from killing while another person is compelled to kill animals for livelihood. Every person would define the concept of right or wrong according to their way of looking at the things. The concept of the right or the wrong cannot be defined in one single and rigid definition. The way you see things is the way you would define them and later on judge them. What holds right for one person may not hold right for other? If we try to bring all the teachings in one single definition; we are definitely on the incorrect path. The judgment of what is right and what is wrong is best left to the individual alone.

## How God judges you?

There is a famous story in the Bible, which clearly establishes the fact that God never choose to punish anyone.

*"...if any one of you is without sin, let him be the first to throw a stone at her."*

Let's not think about the adultery for a moment. God could have punished the woman severely, but chose not to. He only warned the woman. It is clearly evident that God never hates nor condemns anyone. No matter what acts we did, moral or immoral, God never judges or punishes anyone.

*Whoever looks at a woman with lust has already committed adultery with her in his heart. – The Bible.*

According to Bible, seeing a woman with lustful eyes, we commit sin. Whether a person is actively involved into adultery or he is only involved into lustful thoughts, in the end, both of them are equally sinners in the god's eyes.

## How do you judge this?

In the past, in some parts of the world, women were stoned to death for adultery. It still happens in some parts of the world today. The question is not why people choose to commit adultery? The question is how people view those individuals who have been caught committing adultery?

Is judging the other person to be evil going to make you lesser evil? The question is not about the adultery alone. The question is also not about finding who among us the greater evil is. The important question is why we are so quick to point fingers towards others. We too, at some point in our lives, have done something that is not right in the god's eyes. The point is that how we can judge others, when at some point of our lives; we had our share of wrong doings too. It's like one liar wants to see the other liar get prosecuted, one murderer intends to see the other being punished, and one molester wants to see another being punished. How could one wrong person throw stones at the other person accused of doing wrong?

How could one sinful judge the other?

No matter how many grave injuries we have caused to others, no matter how hurtful we were at some point of time in our lives, and no matter we had committed adultery ourselves at some point of our lives, we point our fingers at others.

It's strange that people who themselves don't shy away from adultery despises the other. One liar hates the other liar, and one drug addict despises the other. It is like hating somebody else for the crime we have committed ourselves. Whether something you did was out of a personal choice or it was a collective decision of all, still you cannot escape the consequences. At some point in our lives, unintentionally or intentionally, we all did something wrong, but when it comes to judging the others; we are very quick to pass our verdict. On the contrary, God never holds any grudges against anyone.

No matter how much we might hate a particular person for his or her acts, God never holds grudges against anyone, and he readily forgives everyone. All the differences between poor and rich, sinner and saint – if at all exist; exists on this earth alone. God loves each one of us equally and without any conditions. It is our own thinking that creates the cages of our sufferings. It's we who lock ourselves perpetually into these cages.

## Think about it

*As Buddha had said, as you think, so you become.*

*If you are constantly thinking of revengeful thoughts, one day you would become a revengeful person.*

*If you are constantly thinking of fearful thoughts, one day you would become a fearful person.*

*If you are constantly thinking of loving thoughts, one day you would become a loving person.*

*If someone is constantly engaged into lascivious thoughts, one day the person would become a lustful person.*

*In the end, though unknowingly, the person who is constantly engaged in lustful thought would become an adulterer in the god's eyes.*

## How do you judge this?

Adultery had existed in the past and sadly it will exist in the future as well. Whatever the reason, we are quick to point fingers at others. When we hear of someone caught committing adultery or something like this on the television, on the radio, and in the newspaper, what is the first thing that comes in our mind? Though it required two people to commit the crime, the woman alone is being blamed for the incident that involved two; this is certainly gross injustice. What do we do when we find someone is caught stealing? Immediately, we point fingers towards them. What is our opinion towards the gamblers, the drug addicts, or the smugglers, we hate them. We hate those who have done something wrong, but we love ourselves despite having done so many wrong things in our lives. The question is not about the adultery alone. Many other similar things exist in this world like killing, stealing, robbing, so on and so forth.

*Is it not true that when it comes to ourselves, we have a different set of definition for morality? Again, when it comes to the others, we have different set of definition for morality.*

Whether it's the fear of being caught or the fear of being punished, no amount of punishment works to prevent the wrong from happening. No amount of fear would deter people from doing the wrong. It is like every time a child steals something he is being canned severely. No amount of canning would stop him from stealing again. Unless change happens from within, a change outside is not visible. *No matter how many times we keep falling down, god is always there to hold us up.* God never hates anyone, no matter how great the mistake is.

God readily forgives.

If the fear of punishment were a deterrent, the world would have been a crime free place today. But the world has not become a crime free place even today. It means that the something else is needed besides the punishment system. Even the most stringent punishments including the capital punishment couldn't prevent the crimes like the drug smuggling, killing, rapes, or the terrorist attacks from happening. Why? When it comes to crimes and punishment, we have massive guidelines and books written. No amount of punishment helps. If punishment alone would have act as a deterrent, the world would have been a crime free place. But it hasn't.

Whether it is a person caught in killing, smuggling, or caught stealing, we are the first to throw stones at others. Instead, we should have a deep look within ourselves to make sure that we have never done anything wrong ourselves. The system of punishment works as a means to instill fear among the people, but it does not address the cause of the problem.

There comes a time when people actually stop fearing punishment. Finally, there comes a stage when people can't be controlled by the fear of punishment alone. The only thing that can stop the criminal activities is a deep introspection. The day everyone introspect themselves and stop searching for the wrong things in others, wrong things will stop automatically. A deep look within gives answers to so many questions. Instead of throwing stones at the others, ask yourselves whether you have a right to do it. Change within will show outside.

Unless you change, nothing will. Unless you stop, nothing would.

*The day we actually stop committing adultery in our minds, adultery would cease to exist.*

When we stop doing the wrong things ourselves, the world would become a better place. We need not search the world for the wrong things. If we have a deep look at ourselves, we find that the wrong things are actually lying within us. The day we stop searching the bad things, bad things will stop from happening. The day we start seeking good things, good things will start happening.

*Till the time we keep searching for faults in others, we would keep finding them. The moment we stop searching for faults in others, is the moment we stop finding them.*

*Unless we stop throwing stones at others, we would continue doing it. The moment we stop pointing our fingers at others, is the moment we would stop throwing stones at the others.*

*Till the time we keep searching sins in other people, we would keep finding them. The moment we actually stop searching for the sins in others, is the moment we stop finding them.*

## God never ever judges you

No matter what food you choose to eat, no matter what the colors of your skin, or no matter you believe in God or not, God never judges you on any basis. Each individual has right to decide what is right for him. A person who comes from one religion doesn't mean that he can't bond with a person with a different belief. In the end, everything is good till people are not forcing their belief on to others. The moment you try to force your views on others, you are wrong. It is best left to the person to decide the way he would like to bond with God. Every religion is good if it is helping you bond with the god.

God never choose to judge between a saint and a sinner, a rich and a poor, and a moral and an immoral. The concept of God pronouncing the judgment, and putting people into the hell or the heaven is a manmade concept. God never puts label on the people as we do. Whether you believe in God, you visit a temple, or you follow the rituals, God still loves everybody equally. It is the people who classify and label other people as moral or immoral, good or bad, or rich or poor. God can always see what you hold in your heart. *In the end, it's our love and faith that takes us to god.*

In the end, it is not the religion that matters. Only faith matters.

## How you judge this?

There is a difference between how people judge and how God judge. People can't help judging each other. When people make judgments about each other, it is succeeded by spread of hatred. For instance, when we find a person in a bad state of condition lying on the road, we jump to the conclusion that he might be drunk. On close examining the person, we come to know that the person is an accident victim. Unless we consider the whole picture, we cannot arrive at the whole truth. We are always quick to give our judgments without taking into the consideration everything.

*First we made division among the people like –*
*You are rich.*
*You are poor.*
*You are from this caste.*
*You are from this religion.*

And, if a division in people was not enough, we divided god as well. It is our god. It is not our god. When it comes to our god, religion, or the way of worship, we believe that we are the best. The truth is that God never judges anyone. God never condemns or punishes anyone.

<u>*How would you judge this?*</u>
*It is our god.*
*It is not our god.*
*It is our religion.That is their religion.*
*Our religion is right.*
*Their religion is wrong.*

## The intolerance

We have become so intolerant that we fight over each other's way of living. It can be the eating issues, the way of wearing clothes, or the way of praying. We fill our hearts with hatred for each other and we teach our children to do the same. More than the child, it's the child's parent to be blamed for sowing the seeds of hatred in the young minds. At a later stage, it becomes very difficult to undo the negative effects of each other.

If we accept a person, then we should also accept his religion. Now, this doesn't mean that you start eating what the other person is eating, but it means that you accept the other person despite their choice of food. The keyword is tolerance. You are free to eat according to your choice, and others are free to eat according to their choice.

People often fight with each other to prove who is right and who is wrong. There are some households where the children are being taught not to talk someone outside their religion. Talking to somebody from another religion is no sin. Many children are taught not to eat outside their caste. Now that's strange, but it is a reality. We teach our children to do things we believe to be good, and our children, in turn, would be teaching their children the same teachings. This vicious circle goes on. We teach our children hatred, and god forbid when our children become terrorists at the later stage, we blame each other.

Religion teaches compassion, tolerance and forgiveness.

## The real problem

The world is already busy fighting with some serious issue like terrorism, drug addiction, poverty, and malnourishment. Wouldn't be it better that we direct all our energies into fighting with these crucial issues rather than fighting over the silly issues? Does poverty, illness, terrorism, malnourishment, and drug addiction have any religion? Is there something like good poverty or bad poverty, good terrorism and bad terrorism? The answer is simple – no.

A person from any religion, caste, creed, race, gender, and any economic status could be affected by these issues. Does illness have any religion? Does disease see the religion of a person before affecting? Likewise, does poverty has any religion, caste, gender, race, or background. It can affect anybody, anywhere, and anytime. Don't we all get equally affected by these things? Unless we see the whole picture, we cannot find the whole truth.

## How do you judge this?

If we did something bad, and then think that God would help us save from the consequences, we are totally wrong. No amount of visit paid to the temple would help. If you murder a person deliberately; do you think that God would save you? Would it help? No matter what you do to please God, it won't help.

## How would you judge this?

*If I donate, God would save me.*
*God always puts me into troubles.*
*If I do this, God would punish me.*
*God thinks I am a sinner.*
*God would punish me.*
*God would put me into the hell.*
*God wants me to suffer.*
*I am a child of a lesser god.*
*God doesn't love me.*

The concept of sufferings is not a creation of God. It's our own creation. We have made the concept of hell and heaven and the concept of reward and punishment. Neither do God judge nor does God punish anyone. The existence never distinguishes between a sinner and a saint. It never chooses to judge people. It never hates anybody.

The sunlight, the air, the water, the earth – no force of nature discriminates between people. The sunlight is available to all the people, the air is readily available, the water quenches the thirst of anybody who drinks it, and the mother earth accepts each one of us graciously. In other words, the existence never chooses between a saint and a sinner, a rich and a poor, or a good or a bad. It can be clearly established that there is a supreme truth that governs the world. The supreme truth is beyond the caste, creed, society, and country. The truth is that there is a universal force that is beyond all the disparities and it never discriminates.

Whether you believe in God or not, whether you pray to God or not, or whether you follow the rituals or not – God still loves each one of you equally. God never chooses to judge people. God never puts labels on people as we do. God never puts anyone into hell or heaven. It's our own evil thoughts that are synonym to hell and it's the good thoughts that equals to heaven.

## How you judge sufferings

Whether you believe in God or not, it has nothing to do with the rewards and the punishment. We did something wrong deliberately and then we think that God would forgive us. Would it work? Would God forgive your wrong doings just because you pray to him? Unless and until we change our belief system, nothing would change. Neither do God reward anyone nor does God punish anyone. It's our own karmas that eventually catch us up.

For instance, if you kill someone on purpose and then think that god would save you. Is it possible? When you are facing the consequences of your own act, is it a God's fault? Is it God making you suffer? We think that if we do something wrong and then chant hymns in the temple or donate some money to the poor, God would forgive us. What do you think? God never sees how many hours do you pray daily, how many visits you paid to the temple, or how much good things you utter. In the end, what you store in your heart alone matters. I may hate someone and still talk to them sweetly. Would it work? God only sees what you hold in your heart.

We think that, *'Oh I did this, and god is making me suffer.'* But this is not true. Some people think that god has punished them with poverty and so they continue to live in poverty. While some people think that God has made them dusky because God wills them to be devoid of love. Sometimes, people keep on suffering because they feel that god wants them to suffer. If a child is born with a deformity or mental retardation, people think that it is because of some sins committed in previous life.

The poverty, the color of the skin, the physical, or the mental ailments – all these have nothing to do with the punishment. In fact, we suffer due to our own wrong concept of suffering. We suffer due to our own limited beliefs. God has nothing to do with what a person think or believe, as far as your belief is in sync with the greater truth. We suffer due to our own wrong held beliefs and then we blame god for our sufferings. In the end, it is due to our own limited beliefs and wrong concept of punishment and rewards that leads us to suffering. God never chooses to judge or punish anyone. He loves everyone equally. He never abandons or condemns anyone.

## Compassion over condemnation

Every religion has taught love and compassion. If we dwell on the positive things of the religion, our whole life would change. No religion has ever taught hatred or killing each other. It's not the question of whose religion is the best; it's the question of who inoculates the teachings in the best way.

The problem lies in the incorrect interpretation of the teachings. We modify the truths according to our convenience and then blame others for our miseries. Unless we see the whole picture, we cannot see the whole truth clearly.

If someone tells a good thing, rejecting it just because it is from the other religion is certainly wrong. We get too attached to our ways of thinking and doing things. Over a period, we develop a feeling that we are the sole custodians of the morality. This blind faith often leads to the downfall. In fact, every religion is upright. Good things do not depend on the source. It's disappointing that we are only intent on learning the teachings from our religion.

## How you judge this?

It's the people, who punish themselves. It's our own karma that catches us up. The concept of heaven and hell is our concept. The concept of reward and punishment is man-made. God never chooses to punish people. God never condemns anybody. He always forgives. It's you, who don't forgive yourself.

We keep carrying the heavy burden of guilt and condemnation on our shoulders. We go on building a vicious circle. We have a never ending list of do's and don'ts, right and wrong, moral and immoral. These things pull us back and we can't move forward in life. We get punished by our own guilt, anger, and negativities. It's our own karma that punishes us.

*All evil begins in the mind first. – The Buddha.*

# *WHY YOU ARE YOUR BEST JUDGE*

## Nobody knows you better than you

Right from the day you were born, one person was always there with you. And that person is none other than you. Whether other people are there for you or not, you would still be there. You would still be you. Often, we don't understand the simple things in life. We complicate our lives and get entangled into a never ending cycle of pain. Whether it's the dress you have to choose for the party, or it's the restaurant for having food, or it is your decision on a mid-career switch, there is only one person you can always turn up to, and that person is you.

If you are unhappy with yourself, then you seek help from others who are also unhappy like you. If you are frustrated with yourself, then you seek help from those are who are also frustrated like you. Likewise, if you are depressed with yourself, you seek help from a depressed soul. The point is that you try to seek help from others who are suffering from the same pain. What would happen? You turn up to a person who is suffering alike you; either you end up being understood, or you are left even more wounded. Why? Imagine what would happen if one blind person is leading another blind person. Both of them end up falling into a pit.

*An unhappy soul would make you more sorrowful. A restless soul would bring even more restlessness. A depressed soul would lead to even more depression.*

Everyone is left more hurt, wounded, and desperate. That's how it ends. You cannot give happiness unless you possess it first. You cannot give love and peace unless you have it first. In other words, you can only give something unless you have it first. That's how simple it is. We go out searching for love not knowing that everybody else is doing the same. Everybody is searching for happiness, love, and peace. Imagine what would happen if two unhappy and desperate souls meet. They would create even more unhappiness and even more pain.

Misery leads to even more misery.

## It's good to be you

It's the people who don't feel comfortable in their own skin. The basic reason why we don't accept ourselves is the early conditioning that we received in our childhood. People around us had taught us how to be somebody else. *Nobody has ever taught us how to be just ourselves.* You have to be this. You have to be that. No one ever took the pain to let us be ourselves. So, finally you try to become somebody else to gain acceptance. The result is, you succeed in gaining their acceptance or you end up losing yourselves. Either way, it's painful to be in somebody else's shoes at all the times. You end up losing yourself. You lose your self-esteem and most importantly the real self.

Have you ever felt that why it's so easy to be ourselves? It comes easy to you. It comes effortlessly. You don't have to try at all. Have you ever thought why? It's because you are meant to be the way you are. You cannot be somebody else. Nobody taught you how to breathe or how to sleep, how to digest food, how to walk, or even how to think. It all came naturally to you. Nobody taught it. Isn't it? It's so easy to be yourselves. You need not pretend to be you. Being yourself is as easy as breathing. But sadly, being yourself can also be one the toughest thing.

## How do you judge your life?

It's our life, so, we should decide what is good and what is not. But sadly, it never happens. Like a baby-bird, who breaks open its shell on its own, and the mother lets the baby-bird to walk on its own, and later on to feed on its own, human beings are never self-dependent. In fact, too much concern actually hampers the growth. Right from the childhood to the end of the life, it's the people who decide things for us.

What I have experienced is that when it comes to making decisions, people decide things for us.

People decide our school, the study-hours, the play-hours, the friends, and the list of the entire good thing are decided in advance. The list is long. Again, the people decide what things should be avoided, what kind of food should be eaten and what kind of the food should be avoided. The college, the choice of stream, or the type of job, everything is pre-decided. Whether going abroad is a better option is collectively decided by others.

Again, people decide the person we should marry. People keep on taking decisions for us. We have no other choice left, but to follow them. The whole life is spent this way. Whether it's the decision to quit a job or continue with it, to switch to another job or to continue with the existing one, or to marry someone, is mostly decided by others. No matter what the decision, it can change the whole course of your life. We should judge less and love more.

*You give little when you give of your possessions; it's when you give of yourself that you truly give. - Khalil Gibran.*

Love begets love and hate begets hate. Love always triumphs over hate. The more we share love, the happier we get. Nobody has ever become poor by giving love and peace. *We never stop loving ourselves despite having done so many mistakes, but the same level of empathy is absent when it comes to others.* The difference between mine and yours is always there.

We all had our share of wrong-doings. At some point of our lives, everybody has regrets, the burden of a wrong decision, the guilt of having done something wrong, or a shady past that could never be rectified. These burdens keep on lingering in our minds. We never really forgive ourselves and others. A point comes when we stop growing and don't let others grow as well. To forgive ourselves and to let go off the past needs courage. When we are wrong, we hardly forgive ourselves, let alone others.

## We lack self-acceptance

Since we do not accept ourselves the way we are; we turn to other people hoping that they would accept us. When people also don't accept us, we become frustrated. To gain their acceptance, we change ourselves. In an attempt to gain acceptance, we forget ourselves. The society never accepts us the way we are. We ourselves never accept ourselves the way we are. As a result, we end up losing ourselves. We end up becoming an alien to ourselves.

The whole thing is - self-acceptance. If I accept myself unconditionally, then I need not turn to people to seek their acceptance. The existence accepts us the way we are and more importantly who we are. The sun, the moon, the air, the water, and the earth, accept us wholeheartedly. God never asks us to be somebody else. He accepts us with all our imperfections. He accepts our strengths and weaknesses alike. We need not become somebody else in order to please him.

Isn't it scary that our happiness and fulfillment lies in the hands of the others? Are we dependent on others for our self-esteem? If a friend has taken an engineering course, we too, want to join that particular course. Again, if he has chosen a mechanical field, we want to join that particular field only. Can we guarantee that we will get the same success? Does our happiness really lie in the hands of others? We frequently compare ourselves with the others, the salary, the bungalow, or the car.

If we are in a better position, we become happy. If the others are in better position, we are envious.

If a big house, a fat cheque, and a luxurious car could make us happy, then all the wealthy people in this world would be happy. But, this is not always the case. First, we run after the money so that we can lead a life of comfort. Then, we run after health so that we can enjoy the comforts of money. The vicious cycle goes on perpetually. We can be happy from the fact that even if our garden is not as big as the others, the garden is still green.

Whether it's a career, looks, relationship, or professional matters, we always want to stay ahead of others. We judge ourselves on the basis of what the others are feeling, thinking, or saying about us.

Even if we can't afford to go on a vacation frequently, we should be thankful that we are enjoying it with our family. Even if we live in a rented house, the best part is we are all together. The problem is that each one of us has been given a different set of question paper to solve. We copy the answers of the others not knowing that each one of us has been given an entirely different set of question paper. Blindly copying the answers would give a disastrous result. We have to know ourselves and we have to follow our own path.

*Your best judge is you.*

No matter how good intentions you have, people would still be judging you by your actions. People like to judge everything. The point is that no one has ever escaped being judged. The best thing you could do is to lead a life without thinking much about what others would say. Life is too short for living someone else's life. Think about it. Nobody can help us find our inner peace and happiness. We can only help us to find the path to inner peace, happiness, and fulfillment. No matter how hard you try, you cannot please everybody all the times.

Again, you cannot succeed in becoming successful, happy, rich, and popular at the same time. There is always a possibility of someone richer than you, someone happier, or somebody more famous than you. You cannot spend your whole life by running after the others. Isn't it? It has to end somewhere.

## Do you trust yourselves with decisions?

It's the unpredictability that makes us fearful. We want to have certainty in our lives but forget the fact that life in itself is uncertain. We certainly don't know what would tomorrow bring. We don't trust ourselves enough, so we seek others' help in making decisions. We go to the tarot card readers, the fortune tellers, the palmist, and the astrologers. Now, I have nothing against them. If it's offering you some kind of assurance or bringing you inner peace, it's well and good. But, it doesn't always work? Let alone the major events; we can't even have our judgments on the trivial issues. It is understandable that for decisions like whom to marry, where to invest, whether to switch to the job, or to move to another city, you can consult someone if you are not very sure of the final outcome.

After all, two is better than one.

Take this example. You are a single mother of the only child. Your child has become critically ill. You are on the way to visit your family doctor for over ten years. You decided to take your child to the hospital knowing well that the physician is best at his job. As you are heading towards the hospital, all of a sudden, you change your mind and take your child to the city's most expensive hospital hoping that the best care would be taken. You were unaware of the fact that you would be regretting the decision throughout your life. Your only child dies mid-way to the hospital. Would you live the rest of the life regretting and blaming yourself? Would you accept it as a cruel fate of destiny?

How would you judge this?

## Where to draw the line?

Like a bungee jumper, you know it best that what height is right for you to attempt a jump. No one else can be a better judge than you. By seeing other bungee jumpers, if you decide to jump from a greater height to a level outside your comfort level, what would happen? Wouldn't it be a disaster? As an individual, you know it better that what you should do and what you shouldn't. Isn't it? You are the best judge to decide what the safe height to attempt a jump is. You know the best, what works for you and what doesn't works.

As a person who is on dieting, you know it best what amount of calories you need, and which food you have to avoid. But, people fail in dieting. They make somebody else as their role model and blindly follow their way of eating. They are adhering blindly the diet chart made by someone else. In few days, you find that the method is not working. In fact, you should know yourself better, your body-type, the rate of metabolism, and the threshold for pain while exercising. It is precisely where we fail. We observe that a person has lost a lot of weight in just few days. Without even thinking for a second, we too, start following their way of eating. It doesn't works. If someone has lost weight, it doesn't mean that you would succeed by following their diet plan.

Blindly following others would give disastrous results. Just because someone took an admission to an engineering college to become an engineer, it doesn't mean you would be able to become an engineer too. A person can carry a lot of weight as he is a weight-lifter. It doesn't mean that you will be able to carry a lot of weight instantly. Until you know yourself well; you won't be able to judge yourself well.

People say that life is a series of choices one after the other. You are here because your choices have led you, and the same choices would take you to where you would be tomorrow. In other words, you have to choose whether you like it or not. You have to face the consequences too. Your way of seeing at things would impact the way you decide the things. It means that your way of judging things would have a profound effect upon you.

Life is like a puzzle; you don't know what exactly lies at the end. But you know just one thing, your choices are ultimately dependent upon the way you see and understand things. It means that we only choose the things we think to be good. *The Bible says that we should know ourselves.* We all came to the earth for a purpose. We took birth to fulfill the unfulfilled, to turn the dreams into the reality, and to love and be loved. The dreams that we want to turn into reality, the deep seated desires, the long awaited cherishes, the yearnings, and the longings need to be fulfilled. In other words, we took birth to fulfill our desires, but we soon find ourselves fulfilling someone else's desires.

Do you remember what you wanted to be as a child? Either you wanted to be a doctor, an engineer, an astronaut, a law enforcement officer, a firefighter so on and so forth. Now, what you want to become? I want to be a doctor because my dad wants me to become one. I want to be a beauty queen as my mom wants me to become one. I want to make my parents dream come true and want to be an engineer. I want to be an army man because my grandparents want me to become one. It's clearly evident that you want to be something, because somebody else wants it for you. I want my son to be this. I want my son to be that. Nobody even bothers to ask what the son wants to become?

Now, there is absolutely nothing wrong in fulfilling the dreams someone else has seen for you. The point is that you are fulfilling the dreams at the cost of your dreams. But, it's not a correct thing to do. You live only once. If this life goes into fulfilling someone else's dreams, when are you going to fulfill yours? What is that one thing you would regret not doing after ten years from now? Would you regret listening to your heart to bungee jump at the Nigeria falls or would you regret complying with people's advice to stay away from the jump? Would you regret marrying the woman whom you love the most or would you regret marrying someone else? Again, would you regret leaving the job where everyone was causing troubles for you or would you regret staying there and endure all the pain?

Life is too short to live someone else's life.

Unless you are free of grudges or burden of guilt, you cannot move forward. Tomorrow never comes. What is today may not be tomorrow. What tomorrow might bring, we can't predict today. It's always wise that we live a guilt-free and a grudge-free life. It's wise that we live a life without any regrets. Life is too short to live someone else's life. Often, we hold onto our past mistakes too tight. We never try to break free from the chains of the past.

Life has to be lived; it's up to you to decide how you want to spend your life. Unless you completely forgive yourself and those who have caused the pain, you cannot move forward in life. You have to forgive others because you don't want to remain stuck into your past. Life must go on. Life is a journey, and the more you travel light, the easier it will be for you to continue.

## How would you judge this?

*What is holding you back?*
*What is stopping you?*
*Why are you not living?*
*Why live with regrets?*

## Stop following

Don't do something because others are doing the same. Don't teach your children to do the same way of doing thing. We never question our way of thinking, feeling, and doing the things. Just because our father used to cut the trees with a wooden ax, it doesn't mean that we have to use the same wooden axe too. Until you look at the things differently, you won't be able to find a different solution. You cannot say what marrying to someone might bring out. Either it could turn to be a disaster or it could be a joyful alliance. You never know what is going to happen the next moment.

You have to find out yourself what is right for you. Sometimes, a decision taken in a five minutes to meet someone might bequeath you a lifetime of pain and tears. No amount of running away would help. You have to judge which option is better for you. Seriously, you have to come out with an option. Once you have chosen an option, you have to stick to it, running away won't help. The whole thing comes down to one thing; we judge things by how we see and understand things. Two different people would see the same thing in two different ways.

A glass filled with half of water can be seen in two distinct ways, half full or half empty. The way you look at the things would determine the way you think, feel, and act. A pessimist would see the world as a horrible place full of horrible people. An optimist would see the world with full of friendly people where everyone is helping each other. It's clear that two different reactions may come out from two different people on the same thing. Our way of looking at the things would ultimately decide what we want to see, how we perceive a particular thing, and why we want to see something in that particular way.

## What if you were to die today?

If you were to die today, what is the thing that would hurt you the most? Would you regret following your heart or following the herd. Would you regret doing what you wanted to do or doing what people wanted you to do? What is the one thing that you want to be remembered? To be great, you have to do something great. And you cannot be great until you don't do what you love doing the most. Do you want to be remembered as a person who fought all odds to follow his heart? Do you want to be remembered as someone who spent all his life following others?

Would you like to be remembered as the one who sacrificed his true love and married someone else? Do you want to be remembered as someone who nearly choked himself to death by working three times over his capacity, so that he could fulfill his parents' wish of enjoying a vacation abroad? Now let me make it clear. Fulfilling your loved ones wishes like a vacation abroad is not at all bad, but at the cost of nearly killing oneself, surely is wrong.

Is fulfillment of one person's dream at the cost of someone else's happiness justified?

## Is this your story?

I might not be happy my whole life. Still, I have to marry you because my parents want me to get married. Whosoever is being approved by my parents; I would marry her. Likewise, you wanted to be an engineer but became a doctor. You wanted to be a chef but became an engineer. You wanted to be a writer but became a teacher. Again, you became a wanted to be an actor but became a homemaker.

If you love acting, be an actor. If you love children, be a teacher. If you love food, be a chef. The world is already full of souls carrying the burden of fulfilling the desires of the others. Why do you want to join their league? Wouldn't be it better that you do what you love to do. When something comes out of your love for it, it is always the best.

You loved someone, but you had to marry someone else. Your beloved did the same; she loved you but married someone else whom she did not love. What is this going on? A total of four lives wasted for living up to someone else's dream? Why not marry the one you love, in the first place itself? For whom you are sacrificing your life? Who would be benefitting from all this? People sacrifice their lives hoping that it would make someone else's life better. Can we really make someone happy by brutally killing our wishes? Is it not a form of violence? To bring happiness to others, you have to be happy first. If you want others to be healthy, you need to be healthy first. In order to share peace and love, you first need to have peace and love within yourself.

## Fulfill your dreams today, tomorrow won't come.

If you want to be an engineer, try to become one right away. What is stopping you? What is holding you back? Why are you dreaming of one thing and doing the other? In other words, life is too short to live on the borrowed dreams. It may be that you won't get another chance to undo the done. On higher plane, the life's circumstances, people, and the events are designed by us. It was our choice to come into existence.

According to some religious beliefs, we come to this earth to fulfill our dreams which were left unfulfilled, to do the things which were remained undone. We take birth to fulfill our desires and longings in this lifetime so that we don't have to come to this earth over and over again. It's called completing the circles of our lives by fulfilling all our desires along with the assigned duties and responsibilities.

It should be everyone's endeavor that no desire remains unfulfilled. One shouldn't be left with the dreams unfulfilled, the hopes left broken, and the wishes gone orphaned. It's clear that besides fulfilling our duties and responsibilities, it's absolutely essential that the person's own individual desires are met. In the pursuit of making everyone happy, we keep sacrificing ourselves. Then comes a point in our lives where we are no longer in a position to sacrifice ourselves. We hurt ourselves unnecessarily by carrying someone else's burden on our shoulders. Is torturing ourselves to the point from where we cannot recover, in the name of making others happy justified? Who is going to gain in the end?

## Is this your story?

Why not try to excel at what comes easily and naturally to you. Why do you want to learn something, and then, excel in it? There are people to whom, studying engineering comes easy. They understand everything easily, the formulas, the algorithms, the algebra, arithmetic, geometry, physics, and everything with an ease. For some people, studying engineering is easy. For some people, studying engineering comes hard. It doesn't come to them naturally. But, still they want to pursue engineering only.

If asked the reason for doing a particular thing, people would reply different things. "Everyone in our family, right from the great grandfather to the grandfather to my father, everyone has been an engineer. So, I would also want to be one." Some people who would say, "My father dreamt of making me an engineer as he couldn't become himself, so I want to fulfill his dream of becoming one."

Some would say, "My friends took admission to that particular engineering course; I didn't wanted to be left alone, so, I too joined engineering." It's strange that people say that they are doing that because everyone else is doing it. Different people come up with different reasons and justifications and excuses.

It's not often that you listen someone say that he is doing engineering because he wanted to do it. Some people find it difficult to learn engineering, but, still they want to become an engineer only. By any means, they want to become an engineer. Suppose you succeed in becoming an engineer, who would be benefitted? Conclusively, nobody would benefit from it. All the efforts, money, and time will go waste. Is it worth doing all this?

## How do you judge the depth of a river?

It's strange that people are willing to pay dearly to learn the things they find it tough to learn. It means that you are learning something first and then doing it. It's the hard way to do the things, learning something first and then doing it. Better do something you never have to learn. If singing comes naturally to you, be a singer. Some people don't know how to sing; they learn it first and then initiate singing. Wouldn't the singer to whom singing comes naturally be better than the learned singer?

Again, some people would argue that there is nothing wrong in learning something. There is absolutely nothing wrong in learning anything. The point is that learning something with putting too much of money and time is really not worth the effort. It comes at a cost, cost of your dreams, time, and energy. Another thing is just because everyone was a singer in your family; you assume that you would be able to sing like them too. Singing is not hereditary. That's the reason why children of all the acting stars don't get as famous as their parents.

Again, there are some people who try to put undue pressure on their children to follow their foot-steps. For the people, it's a matter of family prestige. For the children, it's an added burden. A doctor's son has to be a doctor, a singer's son has to be a singer, and an actor's son has to be an actor. Who said it? Your parents did what came naturally to them; you do what comes naturally to you, and let your children live the way they want to live.

## Don't follow. Start living.

Start doing things you love to do. Start judging yourself with your eyes. Start living all over again. If you love making food, go ahead, be a chef. What is stopping you? If acting comes naturally to you, be an actor. Why do you want to learn acting first and then become an actor? Why not do something that comes naturally to you? Why want to be a learned fool?

People don't fail because they don't have potential. People fail because they try to be like others.I would want to be like her. She is my icon. What are we doing, we are just following people blindly? Does it work? The whole problem is that we see ourselves with the perspective of others' eyes. We never see ourselves with our own eyes. In fact, we are our own best judge. You are the best judge to decide what should be done and what shouldn't be. You are the judge to decide what career should be pursued by you and what shouldn't be. You are the judge to decide whom to marry and whom not to. In the end, it is your life altogether.

*You can be good by following the others, but you would be great by following yourselves.*

Your childhood dream was to become a modern farmer by employing scientific and modern equipment. A dream is a dream; be it anything. If you become a modern farmer, show courage by fighting it all the way through the people adverse to your idea, strive to be the best. Likewise, if you want to be a chef, be the best chef in your area. In the same way, if you love stitching, try to be the best tailor in your field. The whole idea is to become the best of what you wanted to become. The whole idea is to prove those people wrong who didn't believe in you, to prove those people wrong who laughed at you. It is all about proving that you were right.

## How do you judge this?

What happens when we see someone acting, we can easily make out that whether acting comes naturally or has been learned. You cannot make someone act naturally. It should come on its own. All you can do is to improve somebody's acting talent so that they become better. People shell in huge amounts of money to join the acting classes hoping that they would become a leading actor one day. Again, I have nothing against these acting classes if they work, but they don't. Acting like the other professional skills should come easy, effortlessly, and on the top of it - naturally. You should be able to act naturally. Nowhere the acting should seem like an acquired skill.

The audience should be able to relate to the actor or the scene. If you are crying in a scene, the audience should be able to feel the pain and start crying. If you are doing something funny, the audience should be able to laugh along with you. That's the power of acting. It cannot be learned. It should come naturally. The reason why many people fail is that they try to learn something first and then do it. If someone is able to do it, it doesn't mean you would be able to do it too. Why you want to join the acting classes first and then become an actor? Why not become what comes naturally to you. Why join expensive coaching classes and pay hefty fees to become an engineer? Why not do something that comes naturally?

## Is this your story?

Would you like to be remembered as someone who sacrificed her dream of marrying her childhood sweetheart to become an actor? Now, one would say that what's the big deal about it? She is getting more name and fame that she never could get by being just an ordinary homemaker? Is that so? On one front, she is fighting with the emotional baggage that comes along the stardom, and on the other hand, she is fighting hard to bury the deep-seated desire to get married and be settled.

Some would say that what special does it take to be an actor, it's so easy. The point is that there's more to actor than just wearing fancy clothes and living a luxurious life. If acting doesn't come easy to you, it's very likely that you would be putting in huge amounts of efforts into portraying a character. The emotional insecurity that comes with the fear of getting it right is huge. Every time you come on the stage, you have to relive all the pain and the emotional trauma while playing particular character. Until you actually feel the pain, you wouldn't be able to project the pain through you.

The important point is, if the acting comes naturally to you, you wouldn't be identifying yourself with the character to such a point that playing it makes you sick. You would be dying for making the scenes appear real even if it costs your health. Again, the crucial aspect is that if you are doing something you don't like doing; you shouldn't be doing it at all.

On the outer side, you are pretending that you like acting very much, and to the contrary, you are resenting being an actor from within. The resentment that would build up within inside will certainly make you ill. And the last thing, popularity comes with a price. You have to sacrifice your family life, your love life, your relations, your friends, and doing the things that fascinate you.

Yes, you sacrifice almost everything for it. And the most important thing is that reaching on the top is one thing and staying there is another. You wanted to be an actor, and you became one, but the story doesn't end here. You have to sustain the position. Getting on the top is one thing, but staying there is what matters the most.

A good actor knows well when to begin the acting and when it has to end. A good actor never carries the character of the film to home. The acting is just a profession and is not greater than life itself. The good actor knows exactly the difference between the character and the real person. The character is not the real person, and the real person is definitely not the character. A good actor feels the pain of the character till a point he is playing a character. That's the biggest difference between a good actor for whom acting comes easily, and the actor for whom acting doesn't comes easily and it requires a lot of efforts.

In fact, both the actors are trying equally hard. For one person, acting comes easily and effortlessly. For the second person, acting comes with lots and lots of efforts. For the latter, acting is like walking on the blade of a knife. Every time there is an attempt to walk, *it bleeds*. The difference can be the difference between life and death; subtle yet fatal enough. The good or a gifted actor knows precisely where the reel life begins and where the real life ends. In fact, if you are someone for whom acting doesn't come naturally, then it's a whole different story. Every shot, every emotion, and every action would require putting in lots efforts. You would be under a lot of pressure. The biggest of all things is the pressure to get the shot right, no matter what the situation is. After you successfully complete a shooting, it is followed by another, then comes another. It goes on. You get trapped into it and come out as a dead person walking. If only you did something that came naturally to you, the story would have been different. If acting doesn't come naturally, every time you act, you are ought to feel the characters pain, and that too, with an extreme intensity.

One pain leads to another. One misery leads to another. One frustration leads to another.

Again, if you are burdened by the ever rising demand of stardom it may cost you, your life. You got to keep up with the momentum or else you would get eliminated. The whole story began with the simple tale of a woman who chose to become an actor to fulfill her mother's wish and it ends on such a pathetic note. The thing is, always strive to do things that come naturally to you. Don't waste your life in living someone else's wishes. Sometimes, it might cost you your life.

## Your heart alone is the best judge

It's always better that you do something that comes easily and naturally to you. You should be master of it rather than trying hard to learn something that doesn't comes easily. It is said that each one of us has been blessed with one good skill that comes natural to us. If someone is a good painter and paints beautifully, we say that painting comes naturally to him. Likewise, some people are fine actors, good chefs, good organizers, good speakers, and good mathematicians by birth. It comes naturally to them. No one ever taught it to them.

Of course, you can hone somebody's singing skills, but what you cannot do is to teach somebody how to sing. Better do what you are good at doing. It is not wise doing something that you aren't good at doing. Don't put too much of effort in unnecessarily learning something. Whether it's the marriage, career, or a major life-changing decision, you are your best judge to decide what is good and what is not.

Nobody knows you better. Nobody can judge you better.

It's always better to follow your heart's longing and be happy rather than following others and resenting throughout the life. It's always better that you do the thing that comes naturally to you. It should come effortlessly. Everything comes down to just one thing – *'easy'*. You don't have to put in effort to breath, it comes naturally. It comes easily.

Likewise, the digestion of food, the blood circulation, and the metabolism, everything happens on its own. You don't have to put in your own efforts. The body's functions are so effortless that they never interfere with your daily activities until the body is ill. Likewise, our dreams shouldn't interfere with our health or our well-being. We have heard so much about self-acceptance. Do we really accept ourselves the way we are? Do we change ourselves following others in order to get accepted? What is the definition of self-acceptance?

The society, the parents, and the elders, everyone tries to mold us according to their way of thinking. There is a strict code of conduct that has to be followed. If you do this, then you would be accepted. If you don't do that, then you won't be accepted. There is an extensive list of do's and don'ts. It should be followed strictly. The conditioning begins early. We are never accepted by the society the way we are. To gain acceptance, we mold ourselves. The society molds us. If you get molded according to people, then you gain acceptance. If you don't get molded by their standards, then you won't be accepted.

If you succeed in gaining acceptance of others, you end up suppressing yourselves. If you succeed in accepting yourselves, you end up losing others' acceptance.

## Practice self-acceptance

Self-acceptance is not something that we read in text books. It's a concept that can be applied in daily practice. People may leave you in your bad times, but it's the inner strength that gives you the courage to move ahead in the midst of turmoil. Criticism, negative talks, and self-doubt hamper our growth. Self-acceptance is all about moving against the tide.

Self-acceptance is the courage to wear the purple lipstick, when everyone else is wearing pink.

It's the courage to be a musician, when people are forcing you to be an engineer.

Self-acceptance is the courage to love the color of the skin without any need for further improvement. Like you don't approve the use of fairness creams but have to apply it.

It's the courage to be single when everyone else is married.

Self-acceptance is all about accepting yourself the way you are without having the need to further improve yourself unnecessarily. Self-acceptance is about having the courage to listen to the inner voice even if everyone is against it.

A person who knows you thoroughly is the right person to judge you. In other words, the person should be aware of everything about you. And, the person who knows everything about you is none other than you. Nobody knows your weaknesses, strengths, likes, and dislikes better than you do. You are your best judge to decide what is right for you and what is not. The time to take charge of your life is now. The person who should be in charge of your life is no one else, but you.

Nobody else, but you are responsible for the present condition of your life. As the driver of the vehicle, he is responsible for the lives of other people he is ferrying. In the same way, whether wrong or right, your decision is going to affect many more lives, other than you. The thing is, you are free to take the decisions but you are not free to escape the consequences. You have to take the responsibilities of your decisions. Unless you learn to accept your decisions, you cannot grow in life.

The more you accept yourselves; the more likely you are saved from the negative effects of the judgments. Self-acceptance is accepting yourself in the midst of the external turmoil and resistance. In fact, it's much easier to accept yourselves when the situation is in your favor but the real courage is shown when everyone is against you. People don't easily accept someone who has the courage to move against the flow of tide. They hate someone who is against the flow. The thing is, self-acceptance is all about accepting yourselves, no matter what the situation is. The more you accept yourselves, the less likely you would judge others negatively.

If we are more peaceful in our lives, we are less likely to be affected by the others negative energies. Likewise, the more inner peace we have in our lives, the less we are likely to be affected by the daily turmoil and the turbulence life tosses at us. In the end, it's our own acceptance and the inner peace that helps us sail through. Whatever you let to grow in your consciousness, it grows. If you let anger, resentment and frustration to grow in your consciousness, it will grow. Again, if you grow love and peace in your consciousness, it will grow as well. After all, the best judge to decide what is good and what is not. You are the best judge to decide your events of life.

You are your own best judge.

# WHAT WOULD BE YOUR JUDGMENTS ON THESE SITUATIONS?

## How you judge this?

You are the head surgeon of a team of surgeons. A critically injured patient is brought in the hospital. The chances of surviving are very dim. The patient is not in a position to stand the operation, but without being operated there are no chances of survival. As a head of the team, it's up to you to decide whether the patient should be operated upon or not. Both the decisions are equally sensitive. Still, the decision has to be taken as the patient's life cannot be left hanging in the loose.

There are some instances in life when you have to arrive with a decision and you cannot escape. You have to directly deal with the decision. It's tough to take decisions in the adverse conditions. The patient's life lies in your hands.

You are the judge to decide what should be done and what shouldn't be done. What's your decision?

## How you judge this?

An insensitive person today, once cared a lot. Now, he doesn't talk to anyone deliberately. He doesn't help anyone even when he is in a position to do it. No matter how much anyone tries to help him, he refutes any help. No amount of persuasion works. He wants to remain indifferent. People are quick to label him insensitive, but nobody cares to find the actual reasons behind it. Once, he was a caring and loving person. He would readily help anyone he could. A sudden twist of fate leads to the unfortunate turn of events. He lost his everything, including his faith in the humanity. What was even more tragic, those people, whom he had helped in their tough times, were the ones who denied him, help. As a result, he became a heartless person. If you see only half a side of a coin and immediately start judging, your judgments would only be a half-truth.

Unless you see the whole picture, you cannot know the whole truth.

How would you judge this person?

## How would you judge this?

You are on a long drive to a vacation. It's a much awaited one. Everything on the road seems to be pleasant. Suddenly a man appears from nowhere and crashes with your vehicle. You are not at the fault, but the man dies on the spot. It's late night and there is no one else on the road. Your primary instincts tell you to run like nothing. You decide to run away. Except you and your family, nobody else knows about the incident. In fact, you should be happy with the fact that nobody else knows about the incident, but you are not. Something is eating you within inside. What would you do? Go to the police station and admit the guilt and face conviction or be tight-lipped about the incident and carry over the burden of guilt all your life. Whatever the decision, the choice is yours. You are the best judge to decide what is the good thing to do? No amount of running away from the truth gives us peace. In the end, it's your decision that either brings you peace or endless worries. No one has ever escaped by running away. The only way is to face the situation.

How would you judge this? What is the right thing to do?

## Is this your story?

Take another case. You are in love with a woman and want to marry her. But, destiny has other plans. Your parents want you to marry someone of their choice. What would you do? You can't make everyone happy at the same time; you lose either way. There is no other way. Either you get married to the woman of your choice and forget your parents or marry the woman of their choice and resent for life. The choice is all yours. You are the best judge to decide what should be done. There is no escape, once the decision is taken.

You can't keep hanging in the middle as a pendulum. In either case, it will be you alone, who would suffer the consequences. Once you are done, means you are done. There is no turning back. There are no re-takes in the real life as that in the reel life. Once decided you have no other choice but to follow the decisions. Life is a hard teacher. There are no fool proof ways to ensure the correct outcome. Nobody can guarantee you results. If you fail in taking correct decisions, it will be again you to suffer the consequences.

In the other words, nobody can escape the consequences. How would you judge this?

## How you judge this?

You see your neighbor helping another woman on a frequent basis. What is the first thing that comes to you? The first thing that strikes in to our mind is that the man is helping her with some poor intentions; it's more likely we would think that there is something fishy going on. Isn't it? Why? These days even helping someone also makes people suspicious. The good is the new bad. Isn't it?

## How you judge this?

You see a young woman meeting someone at the odd hours. What do you think of it? We saw a woman for few second; we don't even know the whole story, but we are quick to judge that she is not a good lady. We judge without thinking. Is it not possible that the young woman is having a meeting with her brother to discuss some very grave issue? Maybe we have customized ourselves to think that way. Not our fault.

How do you judge the whole story?

## What's your judgment about this?

We see a man dressed shoddily with untidy hair and of poor health. He asks for some help. Fearing that he might steal something, we reluctantly help him, but we remain wary of him for the duration we helped him. Why? Do outer appearances matter so much that we think twice before helping someone? Are clothes the only thing that matters? Can good clothes make you a good person and bad clothes make you bad? Does the inner beauty mean nothing?

Without taking into the consideration the whole picture, we jump to conclude that a poor man has to be a thief, too. In fact, stealing is not solely the domain of poor people alone. Even rich people can steal. But, without any basis, we have formed certain notions that rich people can't steal and poor people have to be thieves. Is there any basis in thinking that poor people have to be thieves and rich people can never steal?

How would you judge this?

## How would you judge this?

We see a girl talking to a boy in secrecy on a regular basis. We are quick to conclude that some kind of affair is going on between them. We only see things we want to see, and we only understand things we want to understand.

How would we judge this?

## How would you judge this?

Consider this, you have two marriages proposals, a rich but not so well educated, and a well-educated but not so rich. Whom would you choose? Whatever the judgment, it will impact your life a lot.

How do you judge this?

## How do you judge this?

If we find a woman dressed untidily, we immediately conclude that the woman is so careless and we are so well dressed. We never try to understand the depth, it may be that she is suffering from any emotional turmoil, or it may be that she is facing some personal problem, or it may be she is not in a sound state of mind. The more we focus on the outer appearances of the things, the less we are likely to reach the truth. Things are not exactly the same as they appear to be.

How would you judge this?

## How do you judge this?

We see a woman reaching late at the parents-teacher meeting. We quickly assume that she is a carless and irresponsible woman and we she can't take care of her own child properly. Then, we continue to think that we are very responsible as a parent, we always attend the meeting on time. We never try to see the complete picture. We see something on the surface and immediately jump to the conclusion.

How do you judge this?

## How do you judge this?

We see a mother and son arguing over an issue on their terrace. Without giving a second thought, we think that how uncivilized way people are behaving these days. They don't have any civic sense. If at all they had to pick up a fight, why on the top of a roof? Can't they quarrel somewhere else. We never take the pain to know the whole story. It may be that the son is fighting with his mother over any relationship issue or it may be on some other grave issue. Without considering the whole picture, we jump to conclude that how irrational some people are.

How do you judge this?

## How would you judge this?

When we see a poor person, what is our perception towards them? We think that these are all a bunch of lazy people who don't work hard to have their needs met. How would you judge this?

Now, the twist in the story is, suppose if you were a poor person and people judge you, what's the first thought that comes into your mind? We start blaming the world for being full of hard hearted people who just see a person in pain and still don't bother. How cruel the people have become?

How do you judge this?

## How do you judge this?

A baby is alone and crying too loudly in the shopping mall, the first thing that comes into our mind is how could one leave a baby in such a crowded place? What a careless mother? Can't she even take care of her own child? How would you judge this?

Now, the twist in the story is, suppose you are the mother of a baby. What would be your reaction? Oh! how cruel people have become? A baby is crying in the middle of the crowd and people are busy in their own affairs. No one has time to look after a crying child. What a terrible place the world is.

How do you judge this?

## How do you judge this?

We see a well to do child being caught stealing in a multiplex. What is the first reaction? The parents are to be blamed. Can't they teach some good things to the child? What a shame. It's understandable that if a poor child steals, but a rich child stealing? How do you judge this?

Now, twist in the story. If you were the mother of the child who stole, then what would be your reaction? You justify yourself saying that the thing was not as costly as people are showing it to be. The matter has been blown out of proportions unnecessarily? How do you judge this?

These are just few examples of how we differently judge people and the situations, and how we would judge inversely when we are into them. In other words, when it comes to others we have a different definition of judgments. When it comes to our own, we have altogether different definition.

## *AUTHOR'S BIO –*

I am a simple person who loves to enjoy the little things in life. I feel writing is the best way to express myself. When not writing, I love cooking food, gardening, practicing yoga, and painting. I believe that life is a wonderful gift to make dreams come true.

www.ingramcontent.com/pod-product-compliance
Lightning Source LLC
Chambersburg PA
CBHW031352040426
42444CB00005B/256